UNCLE ROBBIE

To Norman Macht, without whose help with
Uncle Robbie's early and Baltimore years
the body of this book would stand on one leg.

-Jack Kavanagh

To Jack Kavanagh,
keen tracer of lost facts and truths,
and discerner of the difference.

-Norman Macht

UNCLE ROBBIE

Jack Kavanagh & Norman Macht

CONTENTS

"It is doubtful that baseball ever produced a more colorful figure than the esteemed Wilbert Robinson. Like Falstaff, he was not only witty himself but the cause of wit in others. His conversation was a continuous flow of homely philosophy, baseball lore, and good humor. He knew baseball as the spotted setter knows the secrets of quail hunting, by instinct and experience."

- John Kieran, *New York Times*

1.

THE BUTCHER'S BOY

Nobody ever called him Wilbert, except possibly his mother. Tight-corseted, middle-class Victorian New England mothers were not keen on nicknames. Some of his boyhood friends called him Billy Fish, because he often had to break off playing with them to deliver fish for his brother, Harry, who had a fish and oyster business. When the passage of time drew him closer in size and appearance to his three older brothers, he was known as Billy Rob, to distinguish him from Fred, Harry, and George. (There were also two sisters, Clara and Fannie, and a younger brother, Edward.) Much later, the baseball world would know him fondly as "Uncle Robbie."

Nonetheless, it was Wilbert they wrote on his birth certificate, unaccompanied by a middle name, on June 29, 1863, in Bolton, Massachusetts. (Six months later, another catcher-manager, Connie Mack, was born thirty miles away.)

Billy Rob's father, Henry, owned the town slaughterhouse and butcher shop. His mother, Lucy Jane Handley Robinson, had her hands full running the big frame house swarming with healthy, active youngsters on the corner of River and Central Streets. Four years later the adjacent township of Hudson annexed Bolton out of existence. In addition to adding the Robinson house to the tax rolls, the action added Fred and George to the Hudson town team. Hudson sits midway between Boston and Worcester, close enough to get the daily Boston newspapers. The men who gathered in the barber shop and taverns could fan the breeze with the latest baseball scores. In 1871 baseball players organized the National Association—the first professional league. New England's love affair with the Boston team began with its entry in the new league. Managed by Harry Wright, the Red Stockings won four of the five pennants before the disorganized league was superseded by the National League in 1876. So there was plenty of baseball talk in town for young Wilbert to absorb in his early, impressionable years.

Billy Fish was a beefy, boisterous, talkative kid. His nephew, Clarence Robinson, remembered hearing tales of his uncle as a schoolboy. "They said he was one of the boys who would stick the teacher in the wood box. I know he was quite fun-loving."

Billy also loved baseball. He would trail after his big brothers when the town team practiced or played a game against a rival town's nine. Billy soon decided he wanted to be a catcher. He had the stocky build for the position, but more important, he yearned to be the field leader, chattering encouragement to the pitcher, moving the fielders around, and keeping everybody on their toes.

When young Robbie was learning to catch, mitts, padding, and face masks were unknown. Some catchers clamped a piece of wood in their teeth, but bumps, bruises, and fractures were trademarks of the position. The pitcher was forty-five feet away from home plate, and most catchers stood almost that far behind it. They caught the ball on the bounce, much as picnic softball players do today. But Billy Rob wanted to move closer behind the batter. He trained for combat against foul tips by rigging a clothesline at eye level and recruiting other kids to throw the ball at the line. As it deflected off the rope, he tried to snare it with his bare hands. Sometimes he missed and wound up with black eyes or lumps and bruises. But he learned how to catch foul tips.

When he was twelve years old, Billy Rob thought he was ready to join Fred, who was called Slim or Skinny despite his husky build, and George on the town team. But they chased him away. Some of the team members, with their flourishing handlebar mustaches, were as old as his father. Undaunted, Billy organized his own team and called them the Town Boys. He had no trouble establishing himself as the catcher and field captain; nobody else wanted the dangerous position and besides, they would have had to lick Billy in a fight to take it away from him. Billy was also an accomplished wrestler who would soon gain the reputation of being able to throw any man in the state. Even into his sixties, he retained much of his powerful physique and looked as though he could still whip most men half his age.

As leader of the Town Boys, he went looking for teams to play. Years later Robbie recalled his first "match" game with some boys in the nearby town of Bedford.

"I went to our liveryman and hired a horse and wagon. We placed boards across the wagon bed and I hauled the whole team over to Bedford, proudly driving the old horse myself."

To recoup the expense, the boys scraped together $1.20 and made a side bet with the Bedford boys. They lost the game and their fortune.

After mopping up most of the juvenile competition they could find, the Town Boys boldly challenged their older brothers' town team. The grownups brushed them off. Most of them worked long hours six days a week. Sunday was game day and they had a full schedule against other town teams.

But Billy Rob persisted and wore them down as only a nagging little brother can do. Finally the town team gave in to shut him up. The only time they could schedule the game was after work during the week. There would not be enough daylight to get in a full nine innings, but the adults figured they would quickly run up a big score and discourage the kids into quitting before it got dark.

On the day of the big game, the Hudson team trotted out on the field in their handsome uniforms and allowed the raggedy, overalled Town Boys the first at-bats. Almost at once a crisis developed. The game had just gotten under way when the Hudson catcher broke a finger on a foul tip and could not continue. There was nobody else to take his place. The two teams milled about, wondering what to do. They turned to the town blacksmith, a respected mediator of civic disputes, for a solution. He thought a minute, then declared, "Let Billy Robinson catch for both teams." And so Billy Rob did.

No newspaper accounts of the game exist, but the event never faded from Uncle Robbie's memory. With glowing fondness he recalled, "I was so steamed up at catching for both teams that I caught seventeen innings and never thought until afterwards that I had not had my at bats at all."

The Boys lost, but they went down gamely, and Billy Rob impressed his elders enough to be invited to join them as a utility player. His brothers considered him too young to catch, but they let him play in the outfield now and then. Billy Rob watched and learned and grew. He stopped growing before he reached 5-feet-9, but he filled out and wound up as the chunkiest son of the family. Billy Rob survived Hudson elementary school, then went to work in the family butcher shop. At sixteen he became the regular catcher for the Hudson team and celebrated his rite of passage to manhood with his first chaw of tobacco. When the pitcher's box was moved back five feet in 1881, Billy Rob moved closer to home plate. Before leaving the meat market for a game, he would cut a thin slice of steak to slip inside his small buckskin glove.

All the Robinson boys remained in Hudson. While Billy worked in the butcher shop and slaughterhouse, Harry purveyed fish and oysters, then became a barber. Fred opened a grocery store and became a shoemaker. George was a caster and Edward worked as a clerk. They all continued to live in the house on River Street until they married. Fred and George continued to play as infielders on the town team, although Fred sometimes hired out to other town teams in the area.

Billy was twenty when his father died. Now the butcher shop was his. but his heart was not in the business. He watched with envy as Fred, now twenty-eight, went away to try his luck in a renegade major league called the Union Association in 1884. Fred got into three games with the Cincinnati team before returning home, where he joined the Lawrence club in the Eastern New England League as captain and second baseman. The Union Association folded after one season.

Professional baseball beckoned to Billy Rob and by 1885 it had seduced him for good. Despite likely family advice to remain in the meat market full-time, he began to show up at the practice sessions of the Haverhill club in the Eastern New England League. By displaying an infectious enthusiasm and perhaps some choice pork chops liberated from the butcher shop, Wilbert Robinson made the team as the regular catcher. Robbie later enjoyed telling how the Haverhill manager had been sold on him when Robbie leaped over a fence in pursuit of a foul pop-up.

A photo of the Haverhill team shows a clean-shaven, heavily built Robinson among his slender, mustachioed teammates. One of those pictured is a pitcher, John K. Tener, who later became governor of Pennsylvania and, in 1914, president of the National League.

A now crumbling newspaper story appeared in the New York Press in November 1913, written by William F. Prince, manager-first baseman of that Haverhill team. Prince had played briefly in the American Association, National League, and Union Association. His account of Robbie's rookie year provides an early description of the Uncle Robbie the baseball world would come to know and love—a greater contribution to baseball history than Prince's own barely discernible tracks as a player.

In the article Prince reminisced, "I remember when Robbie came into our midst. He was a young, fat butcher boy and...came to us looking like a choice cut of sirloin, fresh as a peach, and he won his way into our hearts with his loving characteristics, which always made up a large part of his makeup.

"From the first day Robbie stepped into the game he was a born leader, though from the position he filled the public perhaps did not suspect it. However, to those who knew him and worked with him, Robbie's worth was always recognized. His constant fire, 'Come on fellows' and ' Let's get at them,' always kept every player on his toes. There were no blues or sulking days with Robbie behind the bat."

Prince recalled that "he was a great catcher from the first day we placed him behind the bat, but to my mind his greatest quality was, and is, his personality. His good nature was a sure remedy to drive away all the blues. No cliques could last while Robbie was around. He taught us to look at all such things as a joke, and drew us together as a sociable, harmonious club."

In July, Frank Selee took over as manager. He was on his way to his greatest achievements, winning five National League championships in Boston, and putting together the Chicago Cubs that would dominate the league from 1906 through 1910.

Haverhill finished third in the standings. Robinson batted .269, good enough to put him among the leading hitters in a dead-ball league in which nobody hit .300. He hit none of his team's seventeen home runs. Robbie returned to the butcher shop and lived with his mother, as he would between seasons for the next few years, but notice had been taken of him in higher circles.

Arthur Irwin was a shortstop who broke in with Worcester in the National League in 1880. He was playing for Providence in 1885 when Wilbert Robinson was catching for Haverhill. At some time during those years, Irwin saw Robbie in action behind the plate. He was impressed by the young catcher's ability to handle his pitchers and direct his infielders during a game. When Irwin moved to the Phillies in 1886, he tipped off Bill Sharsig, who owned and sometimes managed the Philadelphia Athletics in the American Association, about Robinson. (Irwin later managed against Robinson's Orioles teams in the 1890s. The only former player whose place of death is listed as the Atlantic Ocean, he disappeared from a coastal steamer in 1921.) In some accounts of Wilbert Robinson's life, he is depicted as longing to play for the Boston Nationals. In others, he is said to have turned down a $1,500 offer to play for them. In any event, we do know that when Sharsig offered him a $2,000 contract, Robbie signed it and was off to Philadelphia as fast as he could lay down his cleaver and pick up a bat.

Sharsig had organized a semipro team in 1880 when he was twenty-five. When the American Association was formed two years later, he resurrected the old nickname used earlier in Philadelphia—the Athletics—and joined the six-team association. With no major league competition in the city, the club prospered.

But that monopoly lasted only one year. In 1883 the National League, which had dropped the Phillies in 1876 for failing to complete their schedule, readmitted them. Sharsig's A's won the AA pennant in '83, while the Phillies finished last in the National League. But Sharsig was never satisfied with his managers. Beginning in 1884, he hired a new one every year and fired each one before the season ended. In each case, he finished the year as his own manager. When Robinson reported in 1886, Lew Simmons was the manager until Sharsig took over two-thirds of the way through the season. Sharsig was a firm disciplinarian, but he cared about the men who played for him, and Robbie thrived under this style of leadership.

A photo of the team shows a lithe young Robinson with a sleek pointed mustache. It is hard to imagine the youthful catcher wearing the XL uniforms of future years. Immensely popular with teammates and fans, he was quickly elected by the other unwed players to a coveted position. He was named the official measurer of bosoms projected by the nubile members of the Athletics' "Ladies Auxiliary," as a covey of the team's faithful feminine followers called themselves.

The twenty-three year-old rookie batted only .202 (two A's regulars hit below .200). But he stole forty-two bases, the highest felony count of his career. His first hit and stolen base came in his debut on April 19 against the visiting New York Metropolitans. After singling in the seventh inning, Robbie moved to third on a stolen base and a wild pitch, and scored on an error. The A's lost, 4-1. Behind the plate his defense was a little shaky. He made two errors and had a passed ball.

His daring on the basepaths led to the embarrassment of being picked off first base by Pud Galvin in Pittsburgh. A future Hall of Famer, Galvin was renowned for his tricky move to catch baserunners. When the red-faced Robbie dusted himself off and returned to the bench, the A's captain, Harry Stovey, the most famous baserunner of his day, shouted, " That sleep will stand you twenty-five dollars, kid." Before the game was over, Stovey himself had been picked off twice by Galvin. After the game the captain

*Young Billy Robinson behind the bat for the Philadelphia Athletics
of the American Association in 1887.*

breezily told the rookie, "Never mind about the fine, kid. The best of us get caught sometimes." The A's finished sixth that season, and Robinson went back to Hudson and cut steaks and chops for the winter. But he was now a bona fide big league ballplayer.

On March 13,1887 the Boston *Globe* reported, "Billy Robinson leaves Hudson for Philadelphia in good condition, 185 pounds. He kept at his butcher trade all winter." In addition to gaining more experience in his second big league season, he was about to acquire a ready-made family. Mary O'Rourke had emigrated from Ireland to Philadelphia, where she married Herman Augustus von Spiegel, son of a University of Pennsylvania professor. Two years younger than Robinson, Mary was surely not one of the "Ladies Auxiliary" of calibrated measurements. She and von Spiegel had two daughters, Hannah, born in March, 1884, and Mary, born in July, 1885. Herman soon died of tuberculosis, leaving Mary with two little girls to provide for. Mary's granddaughters, Kathleen Hunter and Virginia Harkins, relate the story of how Mary and Robinson met. The widow von Spiegel and Hannah were out walking in the park in Germantown one summer day in 1888 or '89. Hannah, who was four or five, saw a jolly-looking man sitting on a park bench. She walked over to him and said, "You have to meet my mother." Sometime during the courtship that ensued, Robinson began to call Mary "Ma." They were married, probably in 1889, in Philadelphia. Mary was Catholic; Robbie was Episcopalian, though he converted to Catholicism later in life, so they may not have been married in church. But his marriage to a Catholic probably caused some estrangement with his family in Hudson. He rarely returned to his hometown after his marriage. A son, Wilbert Robinson Jr., was born in Philadelphia on June 20, 1890.

In *The Real McGraw*, Blanche McGraw describes this get-acquainted conversation between the eighteen-year-old John McGraw and the twenty-eight year-old Robinson in Baltimore in 1891:

McGraw: "How many kids do you have?"

Robinson: "Four, all devils. Their mother's Irish."

McGraw: "What's her name?"

Robinson: "Mary, but I've always called her Ma."

(There were only three children at the time of this purported exchange; so much for the reliability of contemporary "first-hand" testimony.)

During his five years in Philadelphia, the A's could finish no higher than third. Robbie's right hand was already taking the kind of beating that would mark many an old-time catcher. (In the days before mitts, most players caught mainly with their "good" hand, using what in later years would become their "glove hand" in a supporting role. Many catchers in Robinson's day wore two thin leather gloves, sometimes variously padded.) Many a night he went to bed with a piece of lemon wrapped around a swollen joint. By 1890, Billy Sharsig's experience in baseball had gone from an 1882 monopoly to teams in three leagues competing for the Philadelphia fans' favor. This was the only season of the Players' League, a brave but unsuccessful effort by the players to rebel against the major league salary cap and reserve clause. Sharsig lost Harry Stovey to the Players' League, but Robinson and his star pitcher, Sadie McMahon, winner of 29 games that year, stuck with him. Late in the season Sharsig raised some cash by selling them to Baltimore, where the Association team had no competition. The depleted A's finished seventh, lower than the other two Philadelphia teams, and suffered badly at the gate. It broke Sharsig, and the entire American Association went out of business the following year.

Meanwhile, McMahon won another seven games that year for the Orioles, and became the team's star pitcher in the '90s, while the move set Wilbert Robinson down in the city he would make his home and the center of his life inside and outside of baseball.

2.

THE ORIGINAL ORIOLES

Baltimore in the 1880s was rapidly becoming a rival to Milwaukee as a brewing center. At one point there were thirty-three breweries supplying the bars and beer gardens of the blue-collar city. Some foamed to a modest head, then went flat. One of the brewers who prospered was John von der Horst, although he too had his share of failures. In 1884 he introduced the city's first light beer, made with rice instead of malt. He called it Cabinet Beer. Another light beer, made by Baurenschmidt and called Dancing Girl, outsold Cabinet. A lesson in marketing lurked therein.

John von der Horst had a son named Harry, who was a baseball crank. When the American Association was formed as a major league in 1882, Harry sponsored the Lord Baltimores. He built a double-decked grandstand, Union Park, near Greenmount Avenue and 25th Street. The park encompassed a drainage ditch in front of the clubhouse, crossed by a rickety two-plank bridge. Third place was as high as the Lord Baltimores ever climbed in the AA. It was von der Horst who named the team the Orioles after the Order of the Orioles, a local social club whose major activity was an annual Mardi Gras style parade.

The Orioles actually played in two different leagues in 1890. After finishing fifth in 1889, they dropped out of the AA and joined the Atlantic Association in 1890. They won the Atlantic pennant on the final day of the season, August 25. On the same day, the

Brooklyn Bridegrooms of the AA disbanded. The American Association released the Brooklyn players and moved the franchise to Baltimore, where von der Horst's players finished out the AA season for the shifted franchise. Robinson arrived from Philadelphia in time to get into fourteen games, one of them a bizarre event that illustrated the haphazard condition the American Association had fallen into.

When no umpires showed up for a September 9 game against Toledo, each team supplied one player to umpire. With the score tied 2-2 after seven innings, the Toledo umpire called the game because of darkness. The Baltimore umpire, disagreeing with the decision, then forfeited the game to the Orioles.

Wilbert Robinson caught for Baltimore as the American Association unraveled in 1891. Having put down the Players' League, A.G. Spalding and his National League barons turned their sights on the AA. They fired a devastating broadside by luring King Kelly, the Babe Ruth of the nineteenth century, away from the Cincinnati Reds, where the aging star was the manager. Boston swiped him in August, 1891, paying him $25,000 through the 1892 season, an astronomical sum for the time, equivalent to Babe Ruth's $80,000 in 1932. The Reds folded their tents and finished the year in Milwaukee.

The Orioles finished third in 1891. Robinson batted .216, the lowest of his decade in Baltimore. But two other events would have an immeasurable impact on his life. On July 30, in Pittsburgh, Pirates manager Ned Hanlon was relieved of his managing duties but remained as field captain and center fielder. And a minor league third baseman, John McGraw, joined the Orioles and played in thirty-three games.

On December 17 the National League succeeded in sinking the American Association with an agreement to take four AA teams, including Baltimore, into an expanded, twelve-team National League.

The 1892 Orioles were dreadful. The folding of the American Association had turned loose an array of players for the National's picking, but the Orioles did not join in the hunt. Nor did von der

Horst want to spend the money to send the team south for spring training. They worked out at Union Park and used the Johns Hopkins University gym when the weather was bad. Robinson reported overweight. He lost twenty-five pounds working out, but he could still be described as portly. He and the hefty pitcher Sadie McMahon would soon be labeled the dumpling battery. Robbie also picked up another nickname, Yank, because of his origins in Massachusetts. He didn't much care for that moniker, because another Robinson, William H., a second baseman with the St. Louis Browns, also carried that tag. "I don't want to be mistaken for the real Yank Robinson," he said. "Five years ago that bird made seven errors in seven chances at second base." The "real" Yank Robinson finished his career with Washington in 1892.

John McGraw, the cocky nineteen-year-old infielder, worked harder than anybody to stick with the team. He did not want to go back to the minor leagues. If there was one thing McGraw did not need, it was more seasoning. More experience, maybe, but he was already spicier than Texas four-alarm chili.

Robinson's good nature and field command earned him the team captaincy from manager George Van Haltren, and a $2,800 salary. All the other players made $2,100.

When the team lost eleven of its first twelve games, Van Haltren, the center fielder and leading hitter of the team, went back to the playing ranks. The club secretary, John Waltz, ran the team for a week of losses while von der Horst pursued Ned Hanlon to take over the team. It was the best baseball decision he ever made.

Hanlon had managed Pittsburgh teams in the National League in 1889, the Players' League in 1890, and the National again in 1891 with no notable success. He was thirty-four when he joined the Orioles, and appeared in just eleven games before devoting himself full-time to managing. Somewhat reserved in his manner, he could exhort his troops with a pep talk, but he was basically aloof as a field general. Nonetheless, he became the most innovative manager of the 1890s, and a developer of other managers.

Hanlon was cast from the same mold as McGraw, Hughie Jennings, and Ty Cobb: always thinking of ways to gain an edge on the field. He studied the rule book as some lawyers read the law—for loopholes. His clubhouse became a schoolhouse. Hanlon was the teacher, but his eager students had plenty of ideas of their own and needed no prompting to do their homework. Seven of the 1896 Orioles were among the Hanlon-led players who became managers.

Hanlon put on a uniform for the last time in 1892. From then on he managed in street clothes. He took over a disorganized ragtag bunch of drunks and carousers who ran up more bar tabs than scores. He began to rebuild by shipping a disgruntled Van Haltren to Pittsburgh for outfielder Joe Kelley. The Orioles lost 101 games that year and finished last, which in a twelve-team league is pretty deep in the cellar.

For Robinson, the one bright spot of the season came on June 10. In a 25-7 rout of St. Louis, he was 7 for 7 with six singles and a double, driving in eleven runs. Nobody has ever duplicated his 7 for 7 in a nine-inning game.

During the winter Hanlon cemented his authority by buying thirty percent of the stock in the team and getting himself elected president. Harry von der Horst was demoted to treasurer. Thereafter, when fans complained to Harry about the team, von der Horst would simply point to the button he wore that said, "Ask Hanlon."

One significant change in the rules took place that winter: the National League erased the pitcher's box and moved the pitcher back to the modern 60 feet 6 inches.

With a free hand, Hanlon reinstated the spring training trip south in 1893, taking the boat to Charleston, South Carolina, in late March. McGraw had impressed Hanlon with his aggressive play, but not his defensive acumen at shortstop. In June Hanlon obtained Hughie Jennings from Louisville to play short and moved McGraw to third base. A blue-eyed, freckle-faced carrot-top who never shut up on the field, Jennings added to the Irish Catholic flavor of the Orioles. Hanlon also added Heinie Reitz, a rookie from California, who quickly established himself as an outstanding second baseman.

On August 16 Robinson caught the first no-hitter thrown from the new pitching distance. Bill Hawke, who as a newly signed amateur with St. Louis had beaten the Birds in 1892, pitched the 5-0 win over Washington. Playing a heads-up, scrappy game with seldom a dull moment on the field, the Orioles climbed to eighth place, doubled their 1892 attendance, and showed a profit for the year.

The Robinson family lived in a three-story row house—the predominant form of housing in the city—at 2620 N. Calvert Street. The affable Orioles captain was as popular off the field as in the clubhouse. He was a member of the Elks and the Improved Order of Heptasophs, a fraternal insurance cooperative providing aid to the widows and children of deceased members. Founded in 1852 in New Orleans, the original Order was open to white males who professed belief in a supreme being. Its emblem was a seven-point star. A split occurred among the originals, leading to the formation of the Improved Order in 1880. At its peak in 1906 it had 4,000 members nationally. Robinson belonged to Zeta Conclave No. 6, one of several in the city.

Ned Hanlon worked through the winter to improve the team. In December he put the last piece in place to launch the new dynasty. He traded two journeymen to Brooklyn for an aging Dan Brouthers and a wee outfielder named Willie Keeler, who, at 5-feet-4-1/2, was deemed too small for major league ball by a host of experts.

The Orioles trained in Macon, Georgia, in 1894. All day and long into the night they talked baseball, creating and practicing plays and ploys and strategies—legal and otherwise—to extract the maximum results from "baseball as she is played," as Hanlon put it. John McGraw worked at improving his fielding. With all the brainwork and dirty tricks they would pull, catching the ball was still a basic requisite for winning. Gradually he improved to the point where the Baltimore correspondent for *The Sporting News* reported that McGraw was handling ground balls "as a wayfarer swipes the short end of a five-cent cigar out of a gutter."

The hitting rampage that began after the pitching distance was lengthened continued in 1894. The Orioles scored 1,171 runs in 128 games, yet did not lead the league in that department. Their team batting average of .343 was second to the Phillies' .349.

An unusual look for an Oriole.
Robbie, Baltimore's popular and dignified solid citizen and family man.

Everybody in the lineup batted over .300. Wilbert Robinson, at .353, was topped by Keeler, Steve Brodie, and Joe Kelley, whose .393 wasn't even good enough to make the top five in the league. In addition to batting .335, Jennings became adept at taking one for the team. In a game in May he was hit by a pitch three times.

The Orioles got off to a winning start on opening day, beating the Giants, led by John Montgomery Ward. Robbie threw out three base stealers and picked another off base. On April 24 the Birds were trailing defending champion Boston, 3-1, in the ninth inning. They scored fourteen runs. Two weeks later they routed Washington, 17-0. The offensive explosions combined with the Orioles' incendiary words and actions on the field sparked baseball fever in Baltimore.

Led by the pugnacious McGraw, the Orioles got into frequent fights with players and umpires. In Boston on May 15, 1894, McGraw and Boston third baseman Tommy Tucker got into a fight during the third inning. In a flash everybody was brawling. The fight spread to the right field stands, where it got so hot a fire broke out. Before it was put out, the stands and 170 buildings in the neighborhood were destroyed or damaged.

But the Orioles were just warming up. The year was merely an overture for the rowdy style of play they would become famous—or infamous—for, and they were still a few years away from reaching their peak. With McGraw leading off and Keeler batting second, they made the hit-and-run a devastating maneuver. If they didn't invent it, they perfected it. They did the same with the bunt.

To aid their game, the head groundskeeper, Thomas J. Murphy, doctored the field with the skill of a Johns Hopkins surgeon. As proud of his flourishing mustache as Earl Weaver would later preen over his tomato plants at Memorial Stadium, Murphy banked the base lines to keep bunts from rolling foul. He stirred a binding substance into the dirt around home plate, wetted it down and tamped it hard until it became a concrete launching pad for Keeler to swing down on the ball and bounce it high in the air—the Baltimore chop. The pitcher's box, which was still supposed to be flat, was a foot higher than home plate. Murphy spread soap flakes around it. When the unsuspecting enemy pitcher scooped up some dirt he wound up with slippery fingers. Orioles pitchers kept dry dirt in their back pockets. (Rosin bags were more than thirty years in the future.)

The entire playing field was skewed. It was downhill to first base and second, up a steep incline to third, and downhill to home. Right field was ragged, full of weeds, rough spots, hollows, and hills. It sloped toward a fence, behind which a stream flowed, forming a perpetual bog. Keeler knew every rabbit path and gully. But the Orioles were not satisfied to leave bad enough alone. Murphy let the outfield grass grow until it resembled a wheat field. Keeler, Kelley, and Steve Brodie hid balls in the gullies covered with grass. When a fly ball fell between them or went over their heads they could pluck one from its hiding place and cut down batters who thought they had a sure double. One day a batter hit a line drive into right center field. Keeler dove into the grass and emerged with a stashed ball which he threw to second. Meanwhile, Brodie flagged down the real ball and threw it in. After making sure that he was not seeing double, the umpire called the runner safe. The league ordered the Orioles to give their outfield a regular haircut after that.

They ran the bases as aggressively as they impeded those who trespassed against them. Sometimes, with a man on third, the third base coach, Bill "Boileryard" Clarke, would distract the pitcher by breaking for home during the windup.

For the next few years a typical Orioles inning would go something like this one against the Giants' Amos Rusie, as reported in the Baltimore *Morning Herald*:

"McGraw bunted and beat the ball. Keeler was hit by the pitcher. Jennings tried to bunt but popped a little fly into Rusie's hands. Kelley flied to Van Haltren. Gleason singled to right, McGraw scored. The Kid [Gleason] started to steal second. [The catcher] feinted the throw to second, then sent the ball whizzing to third to catch Keeler who was playing off. Davis let the ball pass and Keeler came home." Two runs on one ball hit safely to the outfield. Another typical scene occurred in the seventh inning of the same game. Keeler beat out a bunt down the third base line. The Giants crowded around umpire John Hunt like a pack of wolves, claiming Keeler was out. "Jack Doyle acted like a howling demon. He grabbed Hunt by the coat and shook him as a terrier would a rat...."

But they could also hit. All season the Orioles battled the Giants and Boston for first place, as the runs piled up. On June 24 Chicago scored five against them in the ninth to take a 10-8 lead. The Orioles scored three in the last of the ninth to claim an 11-10 victory. Over a twenty-four-game stretch they scored at least seven runs a game, and launched an eighteen-game winning streak that kept them at the top of the standings. Steve Brodie was 6 for 6 in one game; Joe Kelley made nine hits in a doubleheader.

Jennings and McGraw shared a room at 12 West 24th Street, near the ballpark. When they weren't playing or practicing, they were talking baseball.

Hungry for a winner, Baltimore cranks flocked to the support of the Birds, embracing them as a future generation would adore a football team called the Colts. After a game they enjoyed the amusement park and beer garden next door to the ballpark, where a band played and von der Horst's beer flowed. Team captain Wilbert Robinson was the most popular player with the fans, who raised money to buy a lot and build a house for him. But the funds were divided among the players at his urging.

As the team rolled through the west, closing in on the flag, an elaborate electric play-by-play board was erected in Ford's Theater. The games were reproduced before packed houses of howling rooters. The newspapers gave the team laudatory, almost worshipful, coverage.The Orioles clinched the pennant on the road and returned home to a boisterous welcome at the railroad station. Bedlam broke loose when the fans spotted Captain Robbie. He and the rest were lifted to men's shoulders and carried to their waiting carriages, which the crowd pulled to the hotel for the public victory banquet.

The revelry that followed the garnering of the twenty-five-foot blue and white National League pennant left the Orioles and their fans with a "who cares" attitude for the Temple Cup playoffs between the champions and the runner-up New York Giants. What did they have to prove by playing the team that had chased them across the finish line? They were the champions. The players were infuriated when they learned that the winners' share would be sixty-five percent of the players' pool. They demanded at least half, win or lose. Their demand got nowhere, but on the practice field before the series began, they found the Giants in a cooperative mood and cut their own deals to split the pot whoever won.

The Orioles lost four straight but went home with more than $625 each. Two nights later, on October 10, the brothers of Lodge No. 7, B.P.O.E., honored Wilbert Robinson at a gala dinner.

3.

1890's "BASEBALL AS SHE IS PLAYED"

The Baltimore Orioles of 1894-1897 have the reputation for being the toughest, rowdiest, dirtiest, most foul-mouthed team in history, unhampered by rules, disdainful of umpires and authority. But they were not unique in their time. Among the twelve clubs of the National League, the Cleveland Spiders were their infamous equals. Led by first baseman-manager Pat Tebeau, who could throw a hip that would fling a passing baserunner into the box seats, they intimidated opponents and umpires fist for fist with the Orioles. Knees, elbows, and extended feet were tollgates to be passed when circling the bases.

When the Orioles and Spiders clashed, they pummeled the poor umpire between them like a badminton shuttlecock. If the pennant had been awarded on the basis of which team was the nastiest and meanest, it would have been a tie. Where the Orioles had the advantage was in their innovations and a superior ability to execute them. They kept a lopsided, mushy ball handy to slip into the game whenever an opportunity arose with the visiting team at bat. They used mirrors to reflect sunlight into the eyes of infielders.

Cleveland may have been their match for dirty play and abuse of umpires, but the Orioles won three pennants in a row and most of baseball's fame and notoriety.

James H. Bready in *The Home Team*, a history of the Orioles, quotes Connie Mack, then the manager at Pittsburgh, as saying,

"The Orioles played the game like gladiators in ancient Roman arenas." They were, in Mack's opinion, clearly "not gentlemen."

In Boston, former player turned sportswriter Tim Murnane called the Baltimore brand of "baseball as she is played...the dirtiest ball ever seen in this country...Diving into the first baseman long after the ball is caught; throwing masks in front of the runner at home plate; catching them by the clothes at third base and interfering with the catcher, were only a few of the tricks performed by these young men from the South."

Honus Wagner remembered a game against the Orioles when he was with Louisville in 1897:

"I hit what should have been an inside-the-park home run. As I rounded first base Jack Doyle gave me the hip. Heinie Reitz almost bowled me over as I passed second. Hughie Jennings tripped me at shortstop, and when I reached third base John McGraw was waiting for me. I was lucky to get a triple. After the game [manager Fred] Clarke gave me the devil for allowing the Orioles to run all over me. The next day I hit a ball down to McGraw at third. I figured it would be a close play at first base. I banged into Doyle with my shoulder and knocked him cold. The ball sailed into right field and I scored. When I reached the bench Clarke was grinning. 'That's the way to play the game, you Dutchman,' he said. 'Make 'em respect you.'"

Umpires dreaded working Orioles games. Tom Lynch vowed he would never work one again, calling them "a vile lot of blackguards." The language they used, he said, would "bring a response in the shape of a bullet if they were off the field."

One day umpire Cy Swartwood had a run-in with McGraw and threw him out of the game. McGraw was wild with rage. After the game he met Swartwood near the bridge that crossed the creek between the stands and the clubhouse.

"I have a notion to take a punch at you," said McGraw.

The ump stuck out his jaw in invitation. McGraw swung and missed. The ump picked him up and threw him into the creek. He lost his balance and fell in behind McGraw. They crawled out and sat, dripping and muddy, laughing at each other.

John Heydler, later president of the National League, called the Orioles "mean, vicious, ready at any time to maim a rival player or an umpire, if it helped their cause. The things they would say to an umpire were unbelievably vile, and they broke the spirits of some fine men. I've seen umpires have to bathe their feet by the hour after McGraw and others spiked them through their shoes."

But not Wilbert Robinson. They never meant Robbie when they recalled those good old bad old days of the 1890s Orioles. McGraw believed that intimidating the umpire would turn some calls the Orioles' way and win some games for them. Robinson, on the other hand, could jolly an umpire with the best of them. He was the salve, the oil, the soothing verbal lotion, the nice one in the McGraw-Robinson good guy-bad guy act. Only it was no act; neither one was playing a role out of character, to be shed once they departed the ballpark. On or off the field, McGraw was truculent, vituperative, foul-mouthed, ready to fight any time. He had the disposition of a man with a permanent pebble in his shoe. Robinson was by nature genial, lighthearted, a friend to one and all, though he could waddle into a brawl when needed.

Arlie Latham, a former player who umpired in the National League in the last year of the Orioles' franchise, described the Robinson-McGraw routine in a *Sporting Life* item: "Robby and McGraw are working both ends against the middle. Robby sleeps in a salve factory and McGraw eats gunpowder for breakfast and washes it down with warm blood. When a poor inoffensive and well-meaning umpire appears in Baltimore, Robinson meets him at the plate, shakes hands with him and remarks, 'I'm glad you came over. They tell me you've been doing great work out west. The boys say you're the best in the business, and between us, I'm glad you're here. These are pretty tough games, old man, and that other fellow we had here was a little to the bad.... You want to watch this pitcher we're trying today. Great lad. Keep your eye on that outside corner. We get lots of them just on the edge and the other fellow missed a lot of them.'

"And all this time, McGraw is barking and snapping around the umpire's heels and threatening to hit him, and if one system doesn't work the other usually does. At least the Orioles aren't getting much the worst of anything."

Who were these rough, tough Orioles, in addition to McGraw and Robinson?

The stationary Dan Brouthers had been moved to Louisville and the Orioles tried rookie George "Scoops" Carey at first base in 1895. Dirty Jack Doyle arrived in 1896 to become the stalwart guardian of first base, complete with bumps and grinds inflicted on baserunners.

William "Kid" Gleason, another 5-foot-7, 150-pounder made of scrap iron, shared second base duties with Heinie Reitz. Gleason is one of the few players to get into a box score in three decades, appearing in one game with the Chicago White Sox in 1912. He is the same Kid Gleason who managed the 1919 Black Sox. Jennings at shortstop and McGraw at third completed the infield.

Johnny Evers, in *Touching Second*, described a play by Hughie Jennings in an 1897 game at Chicago:

"The crowd had encircled the playing field, and was surging closer and closer to the base lines as the battle progressed and, when the ninth inning came with the score tied, one out and Bill Everett on third base, it looked as if Chicago had won…. The batter hit a foul ball, high, and into the crowd back of third base, a crowd ten deep, part seated, part kneeling with rows of standing spectators behind. Jennings, tearing across from short, did not hesitate. Hurling himself through the air he caught the ball over the heads of the spectators and plunged down upon them. Everett meantime had touched third base, turned and was sprinting for home. Jennings, climbing upon the heads and bodies of prostrate spectators, threw to the plate, cut off Everett and in the next inning Baltimore won the game."

Left fielder Joe Kelley was a handsome, well-to-do New Englander who drew the ladies to the bleachers. He could run and hit, and had an arm that averaged twenty assists a year. Handsome Joe carried a small mirror for mid-game sprucing. The cleanup slugger, he scored 167 runs in 1896.

In center field was Walter Scott Brodie, tagged Steve after the daredevil who leaped off the Brooklyn Bridge and lived to boast about it. The son of a Confederate cavalry officer from Virginia, he amused the bleacher fans by singing or talking to the ball, or to himself, almost nonstop. The only time he fell silent was when he made an error and, as the Baltimore *Sun* reported, "as further punishment, he refused to speak to himself during the rest of the game."

One day Brodie took exception to a foghorn-voiced fan who was riding him throughout the game from the left field bleachers. When he'd had enough, he ran from his center field position to the scoreboard in right, grabbed the ladder used to post the scores, and carried it to the bleachers. By the time he climbed to the seats, the raucous fan was headed for the exit. Brodie chased him out of the stands and through the streets before returning to his position.

Brodie was an excellent fielder. He cut the leather out of the center of his tiny glove, preferring to catch the ball with his bare palm. He enjoyed catching fly balls behind his back while facing the bleachers.

Wee Willie Keeler roamed right field, which was probably the best place for him. He would not have fit in with the querulous quartet of the infield. Throwing hips and hurling epithets was not his style. He didn't fight or swear or drink. He had fun playing the game. On the Fourth of July in 1896 he fired blanks in the outfield from a pistol he carried in his back pocket. A so-called bad-ball hitter, especially with a man on first, he would reach up or down or in or out to poke a pitch through the infield.

Keeler's bat-handling feats overshadow his exploits in the outfield. Johnny Evers, who called the Orioles "a team of only fair players winning by dash, nerve, and courage," described Keeler's daring play in a game against Boston. The right field fence, while straight on the outside, sloped at an angle of about sixty-five degrees inside the park. Late in the game, with men on base, Chick Stahl of Boston hit a long fly to right.

"Keeler, one of the fleetest men in the business, seeing the ball was going over his head, leaped upon the slope of the fence and started to run along it, going higher and higher, and just as the ball was going over the fence he caught it. His momentum carried him higher along the incline and before the big crowd realized he had caught the ball, he was running along the top of the fence, and then, holding the ball aloft, he plunged over and fell outside the grounds. Probably never a ball player received such an outburst of applause as he did when he climbed over the fence and tossed the ball to the infield."

In 1897 barbed wire was strung atop the boards in front of the bleachers. Charlie Abbey of Washington hit a drive that was headed over the fence. Keeler raced over, leaped, stuck his bare hand between the strands of wire, and caught the ball as it came down. His arm was cut open as he pulled it back, but he held onto the ball.

The Orioles' leading pitcher of their glory years gets less notice than anybody on the team. Bill Hoffer, a 5-foot-9, 155-pound righthander from Iowa, made his major league debut in 1895 and won thirty-one games against six losses. He was 25-7 in 1896 and 22-11 in '97, but when he went 0-4 to start the '98 season, he was cut loose. Dropped to the minors, he reappeared to hurl the American League's inaugural game for Cleveland at Chicago on April 24, 1901. He became the first American League pitcher to record a base on balls, a strikeout, and a loss.

The more colorful pitchers included Sadie McMahon, a beefy, hard-drinking fastballer who had accompanied Robinson from Philadelphia in 1890; Arlie "Doc" Pond, a credentialed physician who served in the Philippines during the Spanish-American War, then stayed and became wealthy in business, and George Hemming, who learned to pitch while working in an insane asylum, and brought a few quirks of his own to the team. Once he lost a shoe while running the bases and stopped to put it on. Later he explained that he had promised his mother never to play ball barefooted. In 1896 Joe Corbett, brother of heavyweight champion Gentleman Jim, won three games, then won two in the Temple Cup playoffs. The champ and Jake Kilrain, who owned a saloon in the city and had fought John L. Sullivan in the last bareknuckle heavyweight championship bout, were often in the stands.

Smart as they were, the Orioles didn't always use their heads, and when they didn't the guy who pulled the bonehead play heard about it. One day Steve Brodie got a long hit with men on base. He stopped between third and home to applaud himself and was tagged out. The other Orioles rode him harder than the fans.

On January 14, 1895, the grandstand at Union Park burned to the ground. The Orioles wasted no time rebuilding and expanding the seating capacity in anticipation of another banner year. The battle with Cleveland for the pennant raged all season and was not decided until the final week. Led by 35-game winner Cy Young, the Spiders matched the Orioles every step and brawl of the way. Overflow crowds turned out whenever they met, but with ten teams soon out of the race, attendance lagged in several cities.

One of the spectators at a game against the New York Giants at Union Park was a fifteen-year-old cub reporter for the Baltimore *News* named Henry L. Mencken. Mencken's father was a part-owner of the Washington club, and young Mencken occasionally went to a game with his father. Sitting in the bleachers, he kept a longhand score, using a notepad. At the end he penciled this line score:

NEW YORK	9 RUNS	–	13 HITS	–	3 ERRORS
BALTIM.	6 "	–	7 "	–	3 "

Many years later, while going through his papers, the famous editor and caustic wit added this note to his scoring: "(This) was my first attempt at reporting. It describes a game by the famous Baltimore Orioles...I remember seeing the game from the bleachers. After it was over I was delighted to find that my report was correct by a late edition of the [unintelligible]." Mencken never again mentioned baseball in any of his prolific writings.

When the Orioles were on the road, Wilbert Robinson kept in close touch with his wife, firing off telegrams between letters. On July 30, to quell anxiety over a rumored train wreck involving the team, he sent a telegram to Ma from Boston: "No wreck everyone here all right false report. Rob." In August, 1895, their second son, Henry, often called Harry, was born. Between 1895 and 1900, they had two other sons, Edwin and George, both of whom died in infancy.

The Orioles clinched the pennant with a win over the Giants in New York two days before the season ended. Robinson wired Ma: "Cheer up Mary the flag is ours. Don't worry about pitchers [unintelligible—telegrams were written out in longhand in those days] Write tomorrow. Give Henry (Harry) a kiss. Rob."

Fans ranging from a group of postal workers to Robinson's businessmen pals sent telegrams of congratulation to the Broadway Central Hotel, where the team stayed for $2.50 per man a day for a room and four meals. The indifference to the Temple Cup playoffs that had prevailed in 1894 gave way to anticipation as intense as what the World Series commands today, because this time Cleveland was the foe.

The first three games, played in Cleveland, were won by the Spiders. The hostile Cleveland crowd edged onto the field as the first game progressed, throwing produce at outfielders trying to catch fly balls and heckling McGraw from behind third base. The Spiders pulled out a 5-4 win with two runs in the last of the ninth. The next day the fans came armed with heavier artillery: bottles, tin horns, and cushions.

It is difficult to say whether the Orioles reflected or incited the citizenry of Baltimore. Either way, their fighting spirit was shared. When the Spiders arrived in Baltimore for the fourth game, a fired-up band of fans greeted them. Players in those days dressed in their hotels and rode in open horse-drawn carriages or omnibuses to the ballpark and returned the same way. Those rides often resembled running a gauntlet. The unprotected, slow-moving vehicles left their occupants vulnerable to rocks and brickbats mixed with defunct vegetables and rotten eggs.

Cleveland survived the ride but lost the game, the only Orioles win of the series. The next day the Spiders closed out the playoffs and were happy to get out of town. The Spiders might have considered splitting the skulls of Baltimore's fans, but not the winners' share of the players' money. The Orioles had to settle for the losers' share of $385.

4.

NINE BIRDS A-PEAKING

The Baltimore Orioles peaked in 1896. They won 90 and lost 39, for a .698 winning percentage that remains the highest ever reached by a Baltimore major league team. They batted .328, hit 100 triples, and ran up 441 stolen bases. And they did it all without John McGraw for most of the season, and without Wilbert Robinson for a month.

More than 200 fans turned out to see them off in March, as they headed to Macon, Georgia. Despite losing the Temple Cup playoffs two years in a row, confidence and swagger had never been greater. They were the National League champions, and as far as they were concerned, that was as high as you could stand in the world of baseball. It was an attitude that McGraw still carried in 1904, when he refused to play the American League pennant winners. To him, that postseason series was no more important than the Temple Cup.

Training began with a mile run around the field on the day they arrived. Steve Brodie carried a load of bats on the run. In a practice game one day Jack Doyle slid headfirst into every base. Wilbert Robinson, carrying excess baggage as always, jogged the mile from the hotel to the field every day. A team photo shows the dark-haired Robbie sporting a full handlebar mustache, one of seven players so decorated.

Oriole toughness was as evident in spring training as during the season. One day a line drive ripped a fingernail from the outstretched hand of Hughie Jennings. He stayed in the meaningless game. The *Sun* reported, "It would take much more than an ordinary hurt to keep the king of shortstops out of a game played by the Orioles."

When the team started north on the annual barnstorming trek home, they left a chilled and shivering John McGraw behind. The chill was diagnosed as typhoid and McGraw did not return to the lineup until August. On the road north the Orioles ran into local teams for whom a match against the notorious Birds would be the highlight of the season. Like a hometown hotshot itching to draw against the legendary gunslinger who rides into town, every local amateur nine wanted a crack at them. The quickest way to become a hero down at the local barber shop was to out-rough and out-tough the roughest, toughest team in the land. At every whistle stop the local fans became more surly and disagreeable when they learned that McGraw, the rowdiest of them all, was not with the team.

Everybody wanted a piece of the champs. The tour was profitable but painful. They played on fields where home plate was uncomfortably close to a three-foot drop into a ravine, where an outfielder might appear to be standing on a hilltop while another was not visible from the bench.

In Petersburg, Virginia, the fans became so wrought up they attacked the visitors on the field, wrestling them to the ground. At one point Robinson must have thought he was part of Grant's army on its way to take Richmond: a one-armed, gray-haired veteran wearing a faded Confederate uniform bore down on him, threatening to throttle him. The Orioles escaped, only to run into another brawl at the hotel. That one ended only after Kelley and Jennings threw one of their assailants through a plate glass door. Rather than preparing them to open the season, spring training wore them out. They limped home and disappointed an enthusiastic crowd of 11,300 rooters on opening day by making seven errors in a 6-5 loss to Brooklyn.

Through May the pitching was bad and the fielding was worse. Then, given enough time to recuperate from spring training, the Orioles began to roll. Robinson, having his best year at the plate, batted .347 in sixty-seven games. Jim Donnelly, thrust into the lineup in McGraw's place, responded by playing over his head, batting .328. In mid-season they added Joe Quinn, the first Australian-born big leaguer, and he hit over .300. Hughie Jennngs batted .401 and was hit by pitches forty-nine times, a record that stood for seventy-five years. More than once he took one for the team to force in a crucial run with the bases loaded.

In June, Robbie took time out to enjoy a game between his Heptasoph Zeta Conclave No. 6 and the Eutaw Conclave No. 276, played at Union Park as part of a testimonial to him by his fellow Heptasophs. That night they presented him with a silver service "for his manly social qualities in conjunction with his talents as a successful ballplayer," said a newspaper item.

Later that month the Orioles went to New York for a series. In one of the games at the Polo Grounds, the nail of Robinson's right little finger was torn off by a foul tip. The finger became infected, but Robbie played on. Only when the digit began to turn black did he take it seriously. The team was in Louisville, the blackness spreading like nightfall, when doctors decided they would have to amputate to prevent blood poisoning. The Baltimore *Sun* reported, "The genial Robby says he will not take anesthetic. He will not enjoy the operation, but will watch it." On July 14 at Norton Infirmary, they cut his finger off just below the first joint. Said *Sporting Life*, "The end of his little finger has ascended to the celestial realms." (Not only do they not play like they used to; they don't write like they used to either.) By now every finger on Robinson's right hand had been broken at some time—several more than once. All the digits were twisted and the joints enlarged.

Despite the loss of Robinson for a month, the Orioles rolled on. They played so hard Jennings' uniform pants were shredded on a slide into first base one day. The players gathered and escorted him to the clubhouse to change. When McGraw returned to action in August, the Orioles won sixteen of eighteen and clinched the pennant with two weeks to go.

Once again the Orioles faced runner-up Cleveland for the Temple Cup. This time they were determined to make up for their two previous postseason drubbings. They had lost eight of the eleven regular season contests to Cleveland, which boasted the league's top hitter, Jesse Burkett, who batted .410, and top pitcher, 28-game winner Cy Young.

Before the Series opened at Union Park, the Orioles played warm-up games against local amateur nines while the Spiders rusted in rainy Cleveland. The Birds won the first three games easily. Robinson starred in Game 3, hitting a double, making three acrobatic catches of pop fouls, and throwing out a baserunner. They went to Cleveland and squashed the Spiders, 5-0. They filled the Temple Cup with champagne and drank it dry before they left town.

The Series did not draw well. The winners received $200 each, less than half the Spiders' shares of the year before. They earned another $80 apiece playing a few exhibition games and appearing in two theater benefits in Baltimore.

Back home the celebrations began with a gala feast at Ganzhorn's City Hotel, the tables arranged in a diamond shape. Another dinner featured a toast by his eminence Cardinal Gibbons. While other National League players, managers, and umpires heaped scorn on the Orioles and called them everything but gentlemen, the hometown fans gazed upon their favorites and saw only the fairest of the fair. Certainly the fans by the Chesapeake were no different from the Cleveland fans by the lake a hundred years later, who cheered on the terrible-tempered Albert Belle as long as he hit home runs and brought them a pennant. So when Cardinal Gibbons raised a toast and declared, "Much credit is due the Baltimore club, not only for their professional skill, but for their personal and moral rectitude," the multitudes shouted amen.

Cardinal Gibbons obviously never went to a game at Union Park.

5.

END OF AN ERA

John McGraw and Wilbert Robinson were looking for a way to cash in on their personal popularity and that of the Orioles in Baltimore. Robinson's long experience in the meat business led him to think in terms of a restaurant with a basic meat-and-potatoes menu. McGraw's interest ran to pool halls and saloons. Finally they decided to combine all those enterprises into a single emporium that would attract the sporting gentlemen with whom they had been associating in other people's establishments.

By the end of 1896 they were ready. They leased a three-story building at 519 North Howard Street that had formerly housed Beach's Saloon. Located across the street from the Academy of Music, one of the city's best theaters, and near the downtown business district, it promised to draw a steady flow of traffic.

But before they began their renovations, McGraw was married on February 3 to a Baltimore girl, Minnie B. Doyle. Robinson was among several of the Orioles who attended the wedding at St. Vincent's church. After their honeymoon McGraw moved into his father-in-law's house, while he and Robbie supervised the creation of the Diamond Cafe.

They spent more than $10,000 creating a unique gathering place. On entering, patrons were greeted on their right by a long elegant bar. The dining room was to the left. Far from the beanery Robinson had envisioned, it was finished in oak, with elaborate mirrors hanging on papered walls. At the rear of the ground floor, Robinson and McGraw installed bowling alleys made of Georgia pine and rock maple, with the latest patented appliance for returning the balls installed by Brunswick Balke Collender.

On the second floor over the dining room they set up a reading room, where all the current sporting papers could be perused at leisure in comfortable lounging chairs. Three pool tables and a billiard table occupied the rest of the second floor, "all of them fitted with the Ives and Daly cushion, something brand new in Baltimore," one newspaper trumpeted. Photographs and lithographs of baseball players, boxers, and other athletes decorated the walls. The third floor housed a gymnasium, lockers, and small meeting rooms that were available for social clubs and societies.

The two hosts were usually on hand to greet and mix with the customers whenever the Orioles were in town. When they were on the road, an electric scoreboard in the dining room depicted play-by-play accounts of the games. A ticker service clattered out results of other games by innings, as well as results at various race tracks.

McGraw spent more time in the billiards room than anywhere else. Both men enjoyed bowling. Once, when McGraw and Robinson were away duck hunting—which was Robinson's love more than McGraw's—their manager at the Diamond, Frank Vanzant, took the worn and splintered bowling pins to a woodworker to be smoothed. Each renovated pin came out a different size. Like cutting the legs on a table until they were all even, the wood turner kept whittling away until all the pins were the same size—considerably smaller than they had started out. Vanzant brought them back to the Diamond and set them up. When the two enthusiastic fowlers saw them they were reminded of the ducks they'd just been shooting, so "Duck Pins" they became, and the miniaturized form of bowling was born.

The Diamond was a huge success from its opening day. For the Orioles, it was a different story. The three-time champions disappointed the fans who expected a runaway race. Some heads had become swollen with success. McGraw took to snarling and cussing at his teammates more than at the umpires, and became a royal pain in the neck to many of them. He rode Wee Willie Keeler to the point that they tangled naked in the clubhouse one day. Nobody moved to break it up. When McGraw was the first to cry "enough" there were smiles among the onlookers. McGraw blamed Dirty Jack Doyle for stirring up trouble. Doyle blamed McGraw. They were probably both right. McGraw didn't spare manager Ned Hanlon, either, accusing him of taking all the credit for winning and deserving none of it

But for all their squabbling, they stayed on the heels of Boston, where Robinson's former Haverhill manager Frank Selee was building a powerful team. At thirty-four, Robbie caught only forty-eight games and failed to steal a base for the only time in seventeen years. Keeler's bat kept them going: he hit .424. Jennings took one too many for the team, and a fastball fractured his skull. It was three days before he woke up. Later in his career he would take two more fracturing fastballs in the head.

The pennant race came down to a three-game series in late September at Union Park. More than 56,000 jammed the park for the three games, breaking all records for attendance in Baltimore. When Boston took two of the three games, its triumph over the bad Birds brought joy to the baseball establishment.

The two teams met again in the Temple Cup playoffs, which had become so meaningless that the National League mercifully put the plan to sleep after the Orioles won four of the five games before small gatherings of indifferent fans. If the players split the money, it came to about $300 each.

With the Diamond netting the partners three times their baseball salaries, the McGraws and Robinsons moved uptown. Robinson bought a three-story stone house with nine rooms at 2740 St. Paul Street for his family.

McGraw and Robinson were working out in the gym at Johns Hopkins University when the battleship U.S.S. Maine was blown up in Havana harbor on February 15, 1898. When President McKinley asked for a declaration of war against Spain on April 25, the war news overtook baseball. Attendance flagged, then sagged,

The notorious Baltimore Orioles, 1898 edition. By this time, Robinson's career as a player was winding down. He sits at lower left. John McGraw, arms akimbo, stands behind him, next to Wee Willie Keeler.

then collapsed under the absence of a close pennant race. The Orioles won ninety-six games and finished six games back of Boston. The two teams were so far ahead of the rest of the pack that ballparks were empty during the last six weeks of the season. Some days the players and workers outnumbered the people in the grandstand.

Harry von der Horst and Ned Hanlon were looking for greener pastures. They may have felt some early tremors shaking their Baltimore franchise. The war had dampened baseball interest and attendance, and the twelve-team National League was proving to be a cumbersome construction. A six-team second division made for too many losing teams. The two men called on Charles Ebbets and Ferdinand Abell, who controlled the Brooklyn club. Syndicate baseball was the game of the day. Club owners owned pieces of more than one team in the league. John T. Brush had an interest in the Giants as well as owning the Cincinnati Reds. Frank Robison owned the Cleveland and St. Louis clubs. In 1898 twelfth-place St. Louis had lost 111 games. Robison decided that St. Louis had a better baseball future than Cleveland, so he shipped Jess Burkett, Cy Young, and other stars of the Spiders to St. Louis, where they would win eighty-four games in 1899. Cleveland, which had won eighty-one in 1898, won only twenty and lost 134 in 1899.

So there were no officially raised eyebrows when von der Horst and Hanlon began negotiating openly with Ebbets and Abell. Throughout the winter they made frequent trips to New York to meet with the Brooklyn owners. By February 1 the deal was all but completed. On Saturday, February 4 , they agreed to the last step, the purchase of the shares of minority Brooklyn stockholder William G. Byrne for $10,000. Hanlon returned home on Sunday confident that everything was settled, and he began the paperwork to transfer the heart of the Orioles to Brooklyn's camp.

He and von der Horst returned to New York on February 7 with the $10,000. Byrne showed up and sheepishly confessed that, after a week of searching, he could not find his stock certificate. Upon hearing that news, the disgusted von der Horst threw up his hands and said he was going home. As far as he was concerned, the whole deal could be forgotten. "These Brooklynites are the hardest people to understand I ever met," he was quoted as muttering. Hanlon calmed him down, and either Byrne found the certificate or the Brooklyn club issued him a replacement. He got his $10,000. Hanlon and von der Horst wound up owning fifty percent of both the Baltimore and Brooklyn clubs. Ferdinand Abell owned forty percent of each and Ebbets had ten percent. The same board of directors governed both teams.

Some newspapers criticized the arrangement, but that did not bother anybody. Hanlon remained president of the Orioles while managing the newly named Superbas, a name the press took from a popular vaudeville acrobatic act called Hanlon's Superbas. Charles Ebbets became the Brooklyn president. Now that they controlled both teams, Hanlon raided the Orioles' nest. He took Keeler, Dan McGann, Jennings, and the two top pitchers, Doc McJames and Jim Hughes, who had won fifty games between them in 1898. Hanlon wanted to take McGraw and Robinson, too, but they refused to leave their prospering business or comfortable homes. Von der Horst got hot about it and threatened to ban them both from baseball. Hanlon persuaded him to let McGraw manage what remained of the plucked Birds.

Hanlon made plans for the two teams to train together. McGraw and Robinson led a group of minor leaguers, castoffs, and prospects on the boat to Savannah for spring training. But McGraw made one acquisition that would pay him many future dividends. He signed a twenty-eight-year-old pitcher from McAlester in the Indian Territory that became Oklahoma. Joe McGinnity had bounced around the minor leagues and semipro circuits for years with mediocre results. Then he developed an underhand delivery and an assortment of baffling curves that turned him into a winner.

The blond, husky iron worker, whose trade earned him the moniker Iron Man before he earned it again by pitching double-headers, had a roundhouse hook that backed everybody in camp off the plate. McGraw and Robinson were afraid that Hanlon, who had the right to raid the Baltimore roster until April 15, would spot him and take him away. On April 6 the Orioles played the Superbas in Augusta, Georgia. McGinnity pitched. Robbie ordered him to stick to his sweeping slow curve and throw no fastballs. Hanlon passed him up, taking the veteran Dan McFarlan instead. Aided by Robbie's tutelage and handling, McGinnity won twenty-eight games in 1899.

McGraw and Robinson enjoyed what they thought of as a good practical joke, and when they could target an umpire, that was tops. Blanche McGraw related the trick they played that spring on a rookie umpire, Frank Caughey. Preparing to leave Savannah for Baltimore after working exhibition games, Caughey tried to have his trunk picked up for the boat ride. But McGraw and Robbie had conspired with the steamship and railroad agents to refuse the ump's luggage. Every time Caughey tried to leave town, he got turned back, and had to return to the hotel for another night. Eventually they lifted the embargo and the harried umpire went on his way. He never umpired a league game.

The state of umpiring in the National League was as bad as the economic state of the league. Jim Gaffney and George Andrews particularly plagued the Orioles. Even Wilbert Robinson, that supreme jollier of the arbiters, couldn't take it. In a game in New York on April 20, the incompetent duo made so many bad calls that Robbie exploded. His comments led to his first ejection in his fifteen years as a player—and a $5 fine.

Baseball owners and players were a nervous lot throughout the 1899 season. The war continued to cut into attendance. The owners were eager to trim the league to eight cities, but they were afraid to tip their hand too soon, because waiting in the wings to move into any vacated territory was Ban Johnson and his upstart Western League. Baltimore and Louisville were among the cities rumored to be on the block, although the Orioles' home attendance reached 123,416, topping the Superbas' figures in Brooklyn. On the road they continued to draw the biggest crowds.

Occasionally the conflicts arising from interlocking ownerships resulted in awkward situations. Hanlon was still president of the Orioles, the team his Superbas had to play fourteen times. In one late-season game, with Baltimore leading , 1-0, Jimmy Sheckard of the Orioles was ejected but refused to leave the field. The umpire, John Hunt, looked to Hanlon in the Superbas' dugout. Hanlon told him to do whatever he had to do. So Hunt voided owner Hanlon's Orioles lead and forfeited the game to manager Hanlon's Superbas.

On August 26 the Orioles were in Louisville. A telegram arrived informing McGraw that his wife, Minnie, had been taken to the hospital with an inflamed appendix. McGraw got on the next train home. The appendix burst and Minnie died five days later. She was twenty-two.

Ma Robinson had been a close friend who kept Minnie company when the boys were on the road. But there was little she or anyone could do to console McGraw. The best thing he could do was to get back into action on the diamond. He and Robinson drove their threadbare troops the rest of the season and they finished fourth. They led the league with 364 stolen bases, won eighty-six games, and finished fifteen behind Hanlon's Superbas, who soared from tenth to first on the wings of the transplanted Orioles.

That winter the Diamond Cafe was the hot stove league head-quarters in Baltimore. The talk focused on when and where the National League ax would fall. Cleveland was a likely victim; the Spiders had played all but seven of their games on the road from July on, losing a stunning 134 for the year. Louisville also was a weak link. McGraw and Robinson felt so insecure in their hold on an NL spot that McGraw became active in trying to revive the American Association. Between bouts of malaria, McGraw raised money to back new teams in Baltimore and other cities. By February 1 it looked as if enough sponsors had been found to field eight teams. Two former Orioles, Joe Kelley in Philadelphia and Hughie Jennings in Milwaukee, were recruited as managers. But when the Philadelphia backers failed to follow through with the required financing, the whole deal collapsed. Finally, the NL cut Baltimore, Washington, Louisville, and Cleveland. Von der Horst and Hanlon pocketed $30,000 from the league's buyout. The other three teams got $10,000 each. The Orioles retained the right to dispose of the Baltimore players.

Hanlon transferred McGraw and Robinson to Brooklyn, but they refused to go. So the Superbas sold them to the St. Louis Cardinals. They didn't want to go there, either. Their hearts and business interests were in Baltimore. The Baltimore moneymen who had been ready to back them in the American Association cast their eyes on the aggressive Ban Johnson. Led by Harry Goldman, one of the sponsors of the many victory banquets and testimonials to Robinson and the Orioles, they persuaded the two players to go to St. Louis for the 1900 season, make contact with Ban Johnson, get a commitment for a franchise in his new league, and line up players to jump from the National League in the fall.

McGraw and Robinson wanted to be legally unencumbered if the opportunity arose. As operators of the Diamond Cafe, they dealt contractually with suppliers and vendors regularly, and they did not want to appear to be breaking a contract with St. Louis when the time came. They also wanted more than the $2,400 salary cap to go to St. Louis. After negotiations that lasted into May, Cardinals owner Frank Robison agreed to strike the reserve clause from their contracts, making them free agents at the end of the season. McGraw demanded and got $9,500, which probably made him the highest paid player in the game at the time. Robinson earned about $5,500. Their unusual success in negotiations speaks to their value as players.

Pat Tebeau, the Orioles' adversary from the Cleveland Spiders, was now the Cardinals manager. His style was so similar to Hanlon's that the old Orioles had no problem fitting in. But the fire was gone. McGraw played a lackluster third base. He batted .344 and stole twenty-nine bases, but at times his attention wandered to the race track across the street from the ballpark, where some of the players were more eager to score on the ponies than on the basepaths. McGraw was his usual nasty, hot-tempered, belligerent self with the umpires, but a few times he might have been seeking an early exit to get down a few bets across the street.

Robinson caught fifty-four games and batted .248. His patience with the umpiring of Jim Gaffney ran out again on September 19 at Brooklyn. He got so exasperated he threw the ball at Gaffney's legs and spewed an outburst worthy of McGraw. Gaffney swung his mask at Robinson before running him. When McGraw, as field captain, refused to put another catcher behind the plate, Gaffney forfeited the game to Brooklyn. Tebeau had quit in August, and owner Robison withheld the final month's pay from most of the players, blaming the team's poor showing on late hours, dissipation, and showing more interest in gambling than playing ball.

During the season McGraw and Robinson had several meetings with Ban Johnson. Johnson outlined his plans to them and assured them that the Baltimore franchise in his newly-renamed American League would be theirs. Mutual admiration was expressed over firm handshakes. On November 12 he came to Baltimore and they signed the papers, then celebrated over a supper of pheasant and champagne. McGraw and Robinson invested in the team and agreed to take additional shares in lieu of higher salaries.

It proved to be one of those marriages that are not made in heaven.

6.

TRANSITIONS

The fact that Iron Man Joe McGinnity pitched for four different teams in four years is not so much a reflection on McGinnity as on the state of turn-of-the-century baseball. Like a Polish peasant who would live in three different countries during his lifetime only because the borders kept changing around him, McGinnity was a pawn of the interlocking ownerships, the American League invasion, and the shifting vistas of John McGraw.

After his 28-17 rookie season in 1899, McGinnity could no longer be kept under wraps in Baltimore. Brooklyn manager Ned Hanlon persuaded himself, as Baltimore president, to move McGinnity to the Borough of Churches. McGinnity went 29-9 for the Superbas in 1900.

When McGraw and Wilbert Robinson were awarded the Baltimore franchise in the American League, the first prize they went after was McGinnity. They landed him with a $2,800 contract. He earned every dollar of it, completing thirty-nine of forty-three starts in 1901, for a 26-20 record in the American League's initial season. In mid-1902, when McGraw moved to the Giants, the human shuttlecock McGinnity went back over the net to New York.

But for now Robinson had regained his prize pitcher of 1899. McGraw spent the winter on the road, persuading National League players to move to the new American League Orioles, while Robbie stayed home and took care of business at the Diamond

Cafe. In addition to McGinnity, McGraw reclaimed lefthander Jerry Nops and outfielder Handsome Harry Howell, who had been shanghaied from the Orioles by Brooklyn in 1900. He picked up outfielder Cy Seymour from New York and Bill "Wagon Tongue" Keister, a 1900 teammate in St. Louis. Keister was the champion "frequent flier" of his time; he played for a different team in each of his seven big league seasons.

On the surface, all was harmonious between McGraw and Ban Johnson when the American League founder came to Baltimore on Lincoln's birthday, 1901, to take part in the groundbreaking for the new ballpark. For Robinson it was a return to the scene of his Baltimore debut. The grounds had been used by the American Association team until 1891. The new single-deck grandstand and bleachers would seat 8,500.

McGraw left the next day for Hot Springs, Arkansas, where he pursued ballplayers and winners at the local racetrack with equal fervor. He signed Jimmy Williams, a fine second baseman, one of the few players Barney Dreyfuss would lose from the Pittsburgh Pirates; Turkey Mike Donlin, one of their fun-loving teammates from the Cardinals, and Roger Bresnahan, who belonged to the Cubs but had spent most of the 1900 season in Toledo. Bresnahan, whose temperament was cast from the same mold as McGraw's, was a pitcher-infielder-outfielder who agreed to try catching when Robinson was sidelined, and became a Hall of Famer at that position. McGraw also tried to sign Charley Grant, a great second baseman who also happened to be black, and pass him off as an Indian. But Grant, who was working as a bellhop at the hotel where McGraw stayed, was too well-known among discriminatory baseball men and the plot fell through.

Robinson arrived in Hot Springs in late March to shed some winter padding and get acquainted with his new pitching staff during the last three weeks of workouts.

The honeymoon between Ban Johnson and John McGraw lasted barely a week into the season. McGraw was so confident that his old pal, Hughie Jennings, would depart his Brooklyn captors and return to Baltimore that he failed to notify the other American

League raiding parties to lay off him. When Connie Mack offered Jennings $3,500 to play for the Athletics, Jennings accepted the offer. Before he signed a contract, though, McGraw persuaded Jennings to renege on the deal and play for the Orioles. Mack refused to relinquish his claim on Jennings, and league president Johnson backed Mack. Furious, McGraw watched Jennings get on the train to Philadelphia, where, possibly to avoid having to play against his friend, Jennings signed, not with Mack's Athletics, but with the National League Phillies.

The much-awaited opening day in Baltimore had to be awaited a little longer, as rain postponed it for two days. An overflow crowd of more than 10,000 enjoyed the Orioles' debut, a 10-6 win over Boston. Ban Johnson threw out the first ball, then three weeks later threw out McGraw for five days, backing up his vows to support American League umpires.

There was not enough salve in all the locker rooms in the world for Robinson to use on the umpires to save McGraw's neck. Robbie did almost as much managing as catching. He caught sixty-seven games, batted .301, and ran the team whenever McGraw was suspended or had to stay home recovering from the nasty knee injury that pretty much ended his playing days.

The Orioles finished fifth, playing just over .500 ball. The league prospered, except for a weak gate in Milwaukee, which was corrected by shifting that franchise to St. Louis for 1902. But attendance in Baltimore was disappointing. The Orioles drew about 142,000, topping the attendance of only the two lowest teams in the standings, Milwaukee and Cleveland. They didn't lose money, but they didn't make enough for McGraw and Robinson to share in any profits.

By the start of the 1902 season, McGraw wanted no more to do with Johnson than Johnson did with him. Johnson backed his umpires, and handed out suspensions and fines to any player or manager who abused them. Strong, dominant, egocentric personalities, John McGraw and Ban Johnson simply could not live together. There were other problems, too. Johnson needed an American League team in New York, and many felt that the Orioles, with their mediocre attendance, would be the right team to make the move. It was known that McGraw had been talking to Andrew Freedman, the owner of the National League New York Giants, who could, with his great wealth and politcal contacts, block AL entry by making it impossible for a new club to find a spot to build a ballpark. Freedman, possibly the most despised owner in the history of baseball, couldn't keep a manager, and was apparently interested in luring McGraw to the Giants. Wheels were spinning within wheels in the explosive Johnson-McGraw relationship.

Still, the 1902 season looked promising for the Orioles as they left Baltimore on March 22 aboard a Merchants & Miners steamer bound for Savannah. Amid the chaos of players signing multiple contracts, and court battles producing conflicting judgments on teams' claims to jumping players, many old Birds had returned to the roost. Outfielder Jimmy Sheckard, who had bounced between Brooklyn and Baltimore in 1901, landed again in Baltimore. Joe Kelley also jumped back from the Superbas. Dan McGann returned from the Cardinals, and outfielder Kip Selbach leaped from the Giants. The practice of American League raiders inducing National League players to sign predated contracts to nullify their NL pacts prompted Ned Hanlon to comment, "If things keep on at their present rate of signing and cross-signing, some of these players will be holding contracts dated years before their birth."

A holiday mood prevailed as the Philadelphia Athletics arrived at the Eutaw House at 12:45 on April 23 for the Orioles' home opener. A large crowd packed the hotel lobby. After the A's ate a hasty dinner and changed into their uniforms, both teams boarded carriages for a parade up Eutaw Street.

When the band struck up at two, the grandstand and bleachers at the ballpark were already filled for the four o'clock game. The grounds crew stretched ropes across the outfield and the standing room quickly filled. The ladies section soon spilled over into the adjacent grandstand. Brightly colored bonnets were even spotted in the standing room area. The final count was 12,726.

Outside the park scalpers made shady profits. Peanut, lemonade, and sandwich vendors lined the streets. It was a beautiful day for baseball, but beneath the gaiety and optimism forces of darkness seemed to be at work. The Baltimore *Sun* warned that the Orioles were under a triple jinx:

"First a cross-eyed colored girl caught manager McGraw's glittering eye in front of the Eutaw House just as the parade was forming. The manager tried to sidestep nimbly but the spell was upon him. Just as the opening march at the field ended at the players' benches, McGinnity ran back to the pitcher's box and plucked up a green flag that was fluttering cheerily there. Many shook their heads dolefully to see the harp of Erin thus uprooted. They thought it boded no good. Finally when Robinson in preliminary practice fell over and broke down the American flag in the fancy circle that groundskeeper Murphy had fixed up in front of the home players' bench, a low moan of apprehension swept through the ranks of the faithful. A spirit of voodoo was in the air."

The bitter taste of defeat began with an 8-1 loss to the Athletics and quickly grew worse. Jimmy Sheckard played in four games and went back to Brooklyn. McGraw released infielder Jack Dunn and outfielder Steve Brodie, both of whom signed with the Giants. Between suspensions and injuries—a bad spike wound sidelined McGraw for a month—Robinson became the de-facto manager. The attendance held up, running about fourth in the league, but rumors of the league's abandoning the City by the Bay for New York, and of McGraw's negotiations to jump to the National League as manager of the Giants, put a damper on the players as well as the fans.

The break came in early July. The dates and details of the transactions vary, but the effects were beyond dispute. McGraw, with a New York Giants contract in his pocket, claimed that he had laid out more than $7,000 for players' salaries the club could not pay. He demanded the directors reimburse him or buy his stock. Club president John K. Mahon bought him out for $6,500. McGraw then swapped his half of the Diamond Cafe to Robinson in exchange for Robinson's Orioles stock, and persuaded other stockholders, including the Reverend John Boland, the priest who had married McGraw and Minnie Doyle in 1897, to sell their stock to the

Giants owners. Just as Brooklyn had done three years earlier, the Giants, now in control of 201 of the Orioles' 400 shares, stripped the Baltimore roster. They took McGinnity, Bresnahan, and pitcher Jack Cronin. John T. Brush plucked Joe Kelley and Cy Seymour for the Reds.

While all this was going on, Wilbert Robinson was attending his mother's funeral in Hudson, Massachusetts. By the time he got back, the Birds resembled the next-day remains of a Thanksgiving turkey. There was not enough meat left on their bones to field a team. Ban Johnson came to town, declared the team forfeited to the league, and borrowed enough players from other teams to play out the schedule. They went 24-57 under Robinson's dismayed leadership, finishing last in the standings. Robbie caught in eighty-seven games, batted .293 and, at thirty-nine, managed to steal eleven bases. His major league playing days were over. He had caught in 1,316 games, then the major league record. Resigned to the Orioles' quick exit from the American League, Robinson bore no ill will toward McGraw. His erstwhile partner was ambitious, while he was content to remain in Baltimore looking after his business interests.

The war between the leagues ended with a peace treaty signed in January, 1903. The AL moved the Orioles to New York. First called the Highlanders, the team grew up to become the Yankees. Meanwhile, Ned Hanlon, disenchanted with life in Brooklyn, yearned to return to Baltimore. He tried to buy control of the Superbas and move them to Baltimore, but Charlie Ebbets saw an eternal future for baseball in Brooklyn.

The Orioles landed a team in the Eastern League and Hughie Jennings returned to manage it. Robinson caught seventy-five games for the fourth-place Birds. Jennings managed the team through 1906, finishing second once, before going to Detroit where he won three straight pennants. Then Jack Dunn took over the Orioles and began one of the most successful minor league operations of all time.

In 1904, life on the road became wearisome for Robinson. His family wanted him to stay home. Young Wilbert Jr., fourteen, was beginning to show promise as a ballplayer. (Junior, however, soon began to suffer chronic illnesses that would be a constant source of worry to Robbie and Ma. He died at twenty-seven on January 6, 1918.)

Robinson enjoyed working with young pitchers, but at forty-one the rigors of catching were no longer fun. On a long road trip in late June he talked openly about retiring. The other players laughed; they refused to take the genial catcher seriously. He was still doing the job and they did not want to accept the possibility of his absence from their ranks. Then a foul tip broke a finger and Robbie decided that it was time to remove his digits from harm's way. His worn and swollen right hand could take no more punishment. In contrast to his protected, normal left hand, all the joints of the right were enlarged, all the fingers twisted and twice as big around as normal fingers. The thumb was the most deformed; the little finger was missing its tip.

Returning home on July 1, he announced his retirement. Club owners, fans, and friends quickly made plans for a dinner in his honor. On the night of July 7 they gathered at the Diamond. The Baltimore Baseball Company presented him a silver loving cup (auctioned off in 1997 for $1,400) and a statue from the players. The love that Robinson inspired among those who knew him is illustrated in the sentiments expressed by club president Moses M. Frank, even after discounting the opulence of language that prevailed in the era of William Jennings Bryan. Frank waxed, in very small part, as follows:

"With a personal knowledge of your many admirable qualities…when we are about to part with you, one of our oldest members, one of whom we have always found to be a tried and true friend, and one who has served us so faithfully and loyally, every impulse of my nature longs to express the many beautiful thoughts that crowd my mind, and my very words seem to cleave to the roof of my mouth, only to linger there and remain unspoken. Of this deficiency I am deeply conscious, and I am at a loss to adequately express the deep and thorough regret felt by all who are in any way interested in the Baltimore Baseball Club at your retirement."

After the speeches, Robbie thanked one and all and vowed that once the finger had mended the Orioles could count on him to be of service whenever needed. They took him up on that once in 1907, when he stepped in and caught a game for the shorthanded Birds. He also stayed on as a part-time coach, working with the pitchers for Hughie Jennings.

The demise of major league baseball in Baltimore affected business at the Diamond Cafe. The Eastern League did not stir up the enthusiasm and hot stove barbering that big league baseball had sparked. Robinson devoted most of his time to the business and also worked in a meat market. He enjoyed the company of former teammates who made the city their home.

Ned Hanlon, retiring to Baltimore in 1907, became wealthy in real estate. Joe Kelley married the daughter of a Baltimore politician and took a job in city hall. Steve Brodie coached at the nearby Naval Academy, managed the bowling alley adjoining the cafe, and later became a caretaker at Municipal Stadium.

Baltimore *Sun* columnist John Steadman, stumping for Brodie's election to the Hall of Fame, came across a newspaper item advising that "Robinson and Brodie were going on a hunting trip into the wilds of Harford County with [seven companions] to shoot partridges and rabbits.

"They left from the Diamond Cafe, with a wagon carrying the following provisions: two gallons of whiskey, four cases of beer, 10 large porterhouse steaks, two rib roasts, three hams, three boxes of cigars, and five cases of canned goods. A good time was had by all."

Robinson remained active in the Heptasophs and the Elks. In 1907 he was a member of the Maryland Home Coming Association baseball committee. The festivities included a reunion of players from the National League championship teams of the 1890s. They played three exhibition games during Old Home Week. Willie Keeler's father was invited for the occasion and Captain Robbie showed him around town.

In 1909, John McGraw asked Robinson to go to spring training in Marlin, Texas, to work with the Giants' pitchers. When the Giants headed north, Robbie went home to Baltimore. He did the same in 1910. McGraw believed in rounding up dozens of raw recruits and giving them all a look. Robinson would be put in charge of seventeen or eighteen pitchers. His job included warming up all of them in the bullpen to get a firsthand look at what they had. In an article in *Baseball Magazine* in the 1920s he recalled, "I did so much of that work that my throwing arm would move in my sleep."

Robinson had a booming, raspy growl of a voice. He enjoyed roughhousing and lusty jokes, but he also had a side to him that was as gentle as a mother. His ability to be whatever each individual pitcher needed was a key to his success in handling them. "Pitchers are a continual study," he said. "You can never learn all about them. But the more you know, the better off you are."

In the spring of 1911 Rube Marquard became Robinson's special project. McGraw had paid $11,000 for him after the big lefthander won twenty-eight games at Indianapolis in 1908. But Rube had turned into "the $11,000 lemon," winning only nine games against eighteen losses since joining the Giants at the end of the 1908 season. Robbie worked on Marquard's control and got him to throw first-pitch strikes. He taught him how to pace himself and how to mix his pitches—in short, how to be a pitcher, not a thrower. Then Robinson went back to Baltimore, and Marquard blossomed, going 24-7 and teaming with Christy Mathewson to pitch the Giants to their first pennant since 1905.

Robinson rejoined the team in August, and stayed on for the rest of the season and the World Series. There are several versions of how this came about, but general agreement on the effect Robbie had on the club.

According to John McGraw's memoirs, the Giants were slumping in August. They were tired, stale, and lifeless, an unusual condition for a McGraw team. Somebody, recalling Robbie's jovial presence in spring training, suggested they invite him to accompany the team for the rest of the year. McGraw telegraphed the invitation and Robinson accepted. They were sitting around the lobby of the Auditorium Hotel in Chicago, sulking after two straight losses to the Cubs, when the roly-poly Robinson blew in

*Robinson worked for old friend John McGraw's Giants for several years, keeping
the club loose, jockeying the opposition, and helping develop the pitching staff that
led the team to pennants in 1911, 1912, and 1913. The men's long feud began after
the Giants lost the World Series of 1913.*

like the wind off Lake Michigan. He took one look at the long-faced lobby sitters and hollered, "Who's dead around here?" He immediately hoisted some of them off their saggy sofas and took them out for a few beers and a good time. The relaxed Giants then cruised to the pennant seven-and-a-half games ahead of the Cubs. "Gloom faded like a bad dream," New York columnist Damon Runyon wrote.

By 1912, Robinson had become a fulltime coach for McGraw. That spring his special project was Jeff Tesreau, a 6-foot-2 righthanded rookie who threw a swift spitter. Tesreau became the league ERA leader with 1.96 and pitched a no-hitter among seventeen wins in his rookie season. Marquard ran up nineteen straight wins before his first loss, and finished 26-11. The Giants won the pennant handily, but again lost the World Series, the second of three in a row.

No less an authority than Christy Mathewson used every word but "choke" to explain the Giants' three straight Series defeats. Writing in *Everybody's Magazine* in 1914, he claimed the team perennially collapsed under the strain, forgetting how they had played the game all season long, tightening up and committing mental as well as physical errors almost daily.

Matty credited the McGraw-Robinson teamwork for one of New York's victories over the Red Sox in 1912, a win, Matty wrote, that cost the great Smokey Joe Wood, 34-5 that year, $500 he had bet on his own team. According to Mathewson, Wood expected to start the sixth game and gave his money to a friend to bet for him, but Buck O'Brien got the start instead. O'Brien, 20-13 that year, was inclined to be wild. McGraw, coaching third base, and Robinson, coaching first, went to work on him from the first pitch.

"Make him keep his foot on the rubber!" yelled McGraw, although O'Brien was doing just that.

"Get on the bases. He can't pitch without a windup," Robinson bellowed.

O'Brien never had a chance in the verbal crossfire. He gave up five runs in the first inning on six hits, balked in a run, and took the 5-2 loss.

On November 1, New York writer Sam Crane reported, "Robbie has severed connections with the Giants. Although Robbie has sold his hotel and cafe in Baltimore, it's his intention to enter the same business again in that city...After taking charge of rookies in the spring in Marlin, Texas he will go home to Baltimore where he has a most interesting family. All of his children are prosperous and they want their father near them."

Nevertheless, when the 1913 season rolled around, Robinson was back with the Giants as they again won the pennant with ease and lost the World Series to the Athletics, this time in five games. Robinson's annual spring training project this time took the form of a twenty-eight-year-old rookie, Al Demaree, whose 13-4 record made the road to the pennant much smoother. But during the ride tempers frayed and rancor erupted, ending on a note that reverberated for the next seventeen years.

Here again, accounts differ, but are not necessarily contradictory. In his biography of John McGraw, Charles C. Alexander cites an article in *Collier's* of April 14, 1951, "Umpire Bill Klem's Own Story," by Klem and William J. Slocum, as a source for his description of the blowup. After the loss of the final game of the Series at the Polo Grounds, McGraw held a reunion for Hughie Jennings and other old-time Orioles at a New York saloon. He invited Bill Klem to come along. McGraw got drunk and criticized Robinson's third-base coaching decisions in the day's 3-1 loss. Robbie snapped back that McGraw's managing had been pretty lousy, possibly costing them a few games, an assessment that other observers later seconded. Whereupon McGraw fired Robinson.

Klem didn't quote McGraw as firing Robinson. He claimed McGraw snarled, "This is my party. Get the hell out of here," and that Robinson showered McGraw with a glass of beer on his way out. According to Frank Graham, New York beat writer and columnist, Robinson and McGraw had been quarreling throughout the season and the row at the party was simply the final blow of the wedge between them.

Robinson himself backed up Graham's observation. He remembered that with an injured Fred Snodgrass at first, he read a motion by McGraw as a steal sign. Snodgrass couldn't run, but a sign was a sign, and Robbie sent him down on the next pitch. The hobbled Snodgrass was an easy out and McGraw fumed, insisting that he had given no steal sign. According to Robinson, the spat ended with McGraw telling him he would be through with the Giants when the season ended.

Robinson was hunting in Pennsylvania when the news of his release by the Giants became public on October 30. He may have returned to Baltimore in time to watch his son Harry, a star running back and kicker for Polytechnic High School, score two touchdowns and kick two field goals in a 20-10 win over traditional rival City College in the big football game of the year. (The athletic heritage extended as far as a great-grandson, Stan Wilson who, like his great-grandfather, was a nine-year-old catcher playing with twelve-year-olds for the Roland Park Midget League Orioles in Baltimore in 1961.) At fifty, Robbie was not interested in pursuing another baseball job.

Meanwhile, after four straight second division finishes in Brooklyn, the newspapers were full of speculation over the future of the popular Dodgers manager, Bill Dahlen. On October 15 the New York *Sun* had Jake Daubert rumored to replace Dahlen. Other commentators expected Roger Bresnahan to get the job. In early November the Brooklyn *Eagle* cast a vote of confidence for Dahlen. There was no mention of Wilbert Robinson. In fact, Brooklyn's first choice was Hughie Jennings, Detroit's skipper. But the Tigers stifled any negotiations by signing Jennings to a new contract. He would remain in Detroit through 1920.

Charles Ebbets had been aware of the troubles between McGraw and Robinson at the Polo Grounds. Once the split became final he contacted Robinson and signed him, ostensibly as a coach. Dahlen did not get the "blue envelope" (which later became the pink slip) until November 17. Robbie's appointment as the new manager was announced at the same time. In Blanche McGraw's version of events, "John arranged to let Wilbert Robinson go, when Bill Dahlen resigned as manager of the Brooklyn Superbas…John never stood in the way of any player who had a chance to manage." The lapse of time between the October 11 party, Robinson's October 30 release, and his appointment as the Brooklyn manager on November 17, casts doubt on her spin of the tale. Although they would see each other often on the diamond, seventeen seasons would pass before McGraw and Robinson exchanged anything but the barest civilities.

It was almost a month after the ending of his deep friendship with McGraw that Wilbert Robinson finally accepted the job Charlie Ebbets was thrusting upon him. He was weighing the challenge of competing with McGraw as a rival manager against the comfort of a substantial private life in Baltimore. Happily for baseball history, Robbie's competitive spririt won out.

7.

ROBBIE TAKES ROOT IN FLATBUSH

Wilbert Robinson was happy to have a new job. He hadn't worried when McGraw cut him loose. His baseball reputation was high, his friends would back him in another commercial venture like the Diamond Cafe if he wished, and he could always return to the butcher's block if he had to. But the dismissal by the man who had been his closest friend and partner rankled. Robinson would always relish a ball field victory when McGraw was his adversary. In some seasons to come, beating the Giants would make up for a losing year. When the situation required a pose of mutual respect, they shook hands for the cameramen, but neither would make the first move to mend the rift.

The jovial, rotund Robinson, everyone's "Uncle Robbie," fit comfortably into the Brooklyn baseball scene. He was like a favorite relative come to live with the family. However, when the new man-ager took over the helm, baseball's tempestuous seas were roiled by the turmoil of the emerging Federal League. The new circuit had been formed in 1914 as a rival major league to the National and American Leagues.

When Charles Hercules Ebbets had proclaimed in 1912, "Baseball is in its infancy," wise guy writers had scoffed. However, some entrepreneurs regarded it as prophecy. Wealthy men who combined business instincts with an interest in sports eyed baseball's rising concrete and steel stadiums and their ever-larger capacities for ticket-buying crowds. They had the capital to invest in a promising business and would achieve celebrity status, like today's lords of the luxury boxes. Denied the opportunity to buy existing franchises, they created the Federal League. Unlike the almost quixotic ventures of the Union Association of 1884 or the Players' League of 1890, the Federal League dealt hands to men who could stay in the game when the pot was raised. They could meet the ante out of the profits of their successful primary enterprises.

James A. Gilmore of Chicago had prospered in the coal business. He was named league president. Closer to home, Robert B. Ward, head of the Brooklyn-based Ward Baking Company, took up the challenge on the home turf of Ebbets and his partners, Ed and Steve McKeever. Ward rebuilt Washington Park, the ball field in South Brooklyn abandoned when the Brooklyn team moved to the new Ebbets Field in 1912.

Ward and his brothers, George and Walter, were determined to make as great a success of their baseball enterprise as they had in baking, where their Tip Top bread dominated retail sales. Although club president Ward denied that his baseball activity was launched to advertise his bakery, the new team's nickname became the Tip Tops. (The National League's Brooklyn team had continued to be called the Superbas long after Ned Hanlon departed. The older nickname, Dodgers, was frequently used, too. With the ascendancy of Wilbert Robinson, a new name, the Robins, was coined. The three names—all of them informally bestowed by the press, not officially assumed by the team—were used during the early years of Wilbert Robinson's reign. Eventually, though, Brooklyn was most often know as the Robins. Collectively, the players were often called The Flock.)

As soon as Robinson was hired, the new manager met with Charlie Ebbets. The Brooklyn president was a self-made baseball man who traced his pedigree back to a boyhood spent around Washington Park. He had run errands and worked himself into handyman usefulness while developing professional, political, and family roles. As team secretary-treasurer, Ebbets was next in line when club president Charles Byrne died in 1898. He became pres-

Charlie Ebbets, Brooklyn's club president and "self-made baseball man."

ident at thirty-eight. Ebbets' rise was a Horatio Alger story that could have been called, "From Scorecard Boy to Club Owner." Adroit as he was at accomplishing his goals with other people's money, the entrepreneur came up short-handed when it had been time to build Ebbets Field. He took in the McKeever brothers, contractors Ed and Steve, as partners. He kept the title of president and was a very active one. Unlike most other team owners, running his baseball club was his only job. He did it full time. In 1914 he and Wilbert Robinson began a working relationship that endured until Ebbets died in 1925. Robbie ran the team on the field and Charlie Ebbets held the press conferences. Trades and sales of players were handled by Ebbets, but always with the agreement of the manager. There seemed never to be friction between them. In later years, Robinson would be caught in a crossfire between the heirs of Ebbets and the McKeever family. But as long as president Ebbets lived, he and Robbie formed a strong and compatible combination.

Brooklyn's most glaring immediate need was at shortstop. It was to remain a perpetual problem for the franchise during the Robinson years and beyond, with only an occasional fading star plugging the hole for a short stay. Not until Pee Wee Reese took over in 1940 would Brooklyn have a star-quality player at the position for a lengthy career.

Ebbets' first transaction on Robinson's behalf backfired. It became a miscarriage in the birth of the Federal League. In 1913, Joe Tinker, once of the immortalized Chicago Cubs trio Tinker to Evers to Chance, had been player-manager of the Cincinnati Reds. Owner Garry Herrmann wanted a new leader and made a deal with Ebbets. He could have Tinker, still regarded as a top shortstop, for $25,000—a large cash value at the time—with a few players included for the sake of appearances. Of this, Tinker would pocket $10,000 as a bonus. Ebbets offered him a contract for $7,000. This was very big money in those days, but competition had raised the shortstop's expectations. Tinker bolted to the new Federal League, where he became manager of the Chicago team and a recruiting agent for the new league. He almost lured Casey

Stengel away from Brooklyn with an offer to play for the Federal League team in Kansas City, Casey's home town. The announcement that Joe Tinker would be the team's new shortstop had impressed the fans even more than the hiring of Wilbert Robinson as manager. When Ebbets could not deliver, the fans blamed him for not offering Tinker the salary he wanted. Baseball fans have always been profligate with an owner's money. To guard his roster against Federal League raids, Ebbets signed players to multi-year contracts. This cost him, but the players he retained would become the nucleus of the team that Robbie would soon lead to a pennant.

One of baseball's belt-tightening decisions was to limit major league rosters to twenty-one players. There would have to be some paring in spring training when the team assembled in Daytona Beach, Florida, to prepare for the 1914 season. Ebbets also raised ticket prices to the highest levels in the league.

Robinson said he would run his training camp the way Ned Hanlon had done it back in the 1890s—as did that other old Oriole, McGraw. The pitchers and catchers reported a week earlier than the rest. The team played itself into shape with intrasquad games, then faced minor league and nearby college teams before taking on major league opponents as the season neared.

Hanlon, whose eminence in baseball was finally recognized by the Committee on Veterans which voted him into the Baseball Hall of Fame in 1996, provided baseball managers, directly or by extension, for generations after the old Orioles had faded. Fourteen players he managed became big league skippers, beginning with Connie Mack in Pittsburgh. From his own Orioles came pennant-winning leaders John McGraw, Hughie Jennings, and later Wilbert Robinson. Shoots from the main stem were the managers developed by McGraw, including Frank Frisch and Bill Terry, who were World Series victors. McGraw could also claim Casey Stengel as a protégé, but Robinson had a prior claim. Casey was on hand to greet the new manager when the team assembled at Daytona.

Most of the players were holdovers from Bill Dahlen's reign. Bad Bill's temperament was opposite to Robinson's. He would tongue-lash players for mistakes and errors. Robbie was different. Rather

Team captain Jake Daubert was the finest-fielding first baseman in the National League when Robinson took over the Dodgers, and he had won the batting title in 1913, to boot. During the Federal League War, he won a five-year contract from Ebbets, who also agreed to eliminate the reserve clause from it. He was traded to Cincinnati in time to play against the Black Sox in the 1919 World Series.

than curse a culprit who threw to the wrong base or failed to back up one, he would put an arm around the errant player's shoulder. "I can't understand how a man who is as smart as you are could make a mistake like that. You know better. Maybe you weren't thinking ahead on the play. Next time show us you are the smart player we know you are."

In spring training it was evident the players preferred the style of their new manager. As the season went along Wilbert Robinson developed great rapport with them. He never lost their affection. His personality was suited for the playing personnel he had to work with. With few exceptions, a Brooklyn player during Robinson's reign was flawed in some respect. Some played despite injuries. Others were over the hill. Some had skills that were off-set by glaring weaknesses. Pitchers seemed to do their best only against certain opponents. Robbie matched his starters against teams they were more likely to beat, a plan that succeeded only when his staff had sufficient depth. His special ability was to meld misfits into teams that challenged for pennants—and sometimes won—when no one expected them to compete.

Joe Tinker never reported to Brooklyn and the players who jumped to the Federal League were unimportant to the team. For a while it seemed that Tinker would not be missed. There was a redheaded rookie in camp, Ollie O'Mara, a scrawny Irish kid from the Kerry Patch section of St. Louis. O'Mara covered wide expanses of ground, had a strong arm, and although mostly a singles hitter, at first hit them frequently. A broken leg cut short his season. At second base Brooklyn had one of the best players in the league, George Cutshaw. A reliable hitter with the knack of using his base hits to score runs, he was more than solid in the field, could be depended on to play smart baseball, and was a durable everyday player.

Third base was handled by Red Smith, a proven player whose hitting would fall off in 1914. He was sold to Boston on August 10, and starred during the Braves' pennant drive, only to break a leg in a late-season game in Brooklyn and miss the Braves' World Series sweep of the A's.

At first base was the gem of the infield, Jake Daubert, who had led the National League in batting in 1913 and earned the Chalmers Award, a touring car from the automobile manufacturing company. Considered the top fielding first baseman of his time, with the exception of the unpredictable Hal Chase, Daubert was the team captain and the good family man the people of the Borough of Churches appreciated. One of baseball's overlooked stars, Daubert had power for his time. He was also a skillful bunter who usually batted second. His career total of 392 sacrifice hits still stands as a league record.

The outfield had two stars: Zack Wheat and Casey Stengel. Both are in the Hall of Fame, although Casey's honor is due to his managerial successes. Wheat was a Dodger favorite for eighteen years. Stengel had played only one full season, but already had won over the fans with his exuberant approach to the game.

There was a well-traveled rookie in camp, brought up from Newark in the International League, a club Ebbets owned stock in, and which he used to develop players and build up a nearby source of reserves. Jack Dalton was an outfielder who had wandered through the top minor leagues after a brief appearance in the American League. In 1914, he was what Robinson wanted for center field. Stengel had played it well the year before but his manager moved him to right, where he wanted a lefthanded thrower, because he contended they could usually get the ball back to the infield quicker than righties. Dalton, who was righthanded, was put in center field and with his exceptional speed covered it outstandingly.

The Dodgers, or Superbas, depending on what paper you read, (the Brooklyn *Eagle* still favoring Superbas) came north with their team set except for the batterymen. They had four catchers, and the former catcher who was their new manager liked them all. Pitching, despite Robbie's reputed special talent to develop it, would be the team's weakness in his debut year. Soon it would become the team's strength. Nineteen-fourteen would be a year of adjustments, but it would also be a year of hopeful progress.

8.

BUILDING A WINNER

When Brooklyn opened the 1914 season, Ebbets Field was still new. Robinson had visited the concrete and steel stadium, a new trend in ballpark construction, as a New York Giants coach. He had sat on the visitor's bench and dressed in the visiting team's locker room. Now he had his own office under the stands.

It was a grand beginning. Robinson marched with his team to raise the American flag in center field, where fans hoped a pennant would soon fly. Shannon's Regimental Band oompahed at the head of the parade and the new manager was greeted with a floral horseshoe. If it was to signal luck, it did so right away. After Brooklyn's new postmaster, William E. Kelly, had thrown out the first ball, Ed Reulbach beat the Boston Braves, 8-2. A newcomer, Jeff Pfeffer, provided some mop-up help late in the game.

Ed Reulbach had been a major star, leading the National League in winning percentage with the champion Chicago Cubs in 1906, 1907, and 1908. He had been a standout on a superlative staff, headed by Three-Finger Brown. When his arm lost some of its zip, he had drifted to Brooklyn in 1913 and was briefly rejuvenated. Much had been expected of Reulbach under the deft handling of his new manager. Instead, he became a storm center off the field. Some blamed his erratic mound performances on his position as an official of the Players Association. Organized to give the players as much advantage as they could get under the reserve clause, which bound them to one team, the Association hoped to use the new Federal League for leverage.

Both Reulbach and Jake Daubert threatened to jump to the new league, which was offering big contracts. Reulbach did depart in 1915. Daubert extracted an unprecedented deal out of Ebbets. The team captain won a five-year contract and got Ebbets to drop the reserve clause from it. In a series of multiyear signings, Ebbets locked in his best players. It was a risk he considered worth taking to preserve the nucleus of his team. As an incoming manager, Robinson was relieved to let Ebbets handle all the contract negotiations. In his debut year as a manager, he had an unsettled pitching staff to deal with.

Reulbach failed to become a consistent leader, ending with an 11-18 record. Nap Rucker, for years the staff's best, had faltered in

The grand, new, thoroughly up-to-date Ebbets Field, opened in 1913 and was inhabited by Robbie for two decades.

1913 and failed to recover his old form for Robinson in 1914. Once considered, in Brooklyn at least, the peer of Christy Mathewson and Three-Finger Brown, Rucker is unappreciated today by those who evaluate players of the past by statistical formulas alone. Even John McGraw admitted that Rucker was the best lefthander he ever saw in baseball. Few pitchers have ever lost so many well-pitched games as this favorite of Brooklyn fans in the years before Robbie took over the team.

Newcomer Jeff Pfeffer emerged as Robinson's first big winner (23-12). He was the second of the Pfeffer brothers to reach the major leagues. Both were called "Jeff" because both were big men, resembling James J. Jeffries, the former heavyweight champion. The older Jeff Pfeffer, known as Big Jeff, had flashed briefly, but a chronic sore arm ended his career as his kid brother's began. Brooklyn's Jeff Pfeffer had three brilliant seasons, led the way to one pennant, and helped win another. While in a Dodger uniform he won 113 games, then increased his major league totals to 158-112 with several productive seasons after his days as one of Robbie's flock.

The rest of the 1914 staff was a ragtag assembly. One, Raleigh Aitchison, proved one of Robinson's beliefs: some pitchers can beat certain teams consistently. He beat the pennant-winning Boston Braves eight straight before losing to them in his final start. Unfortunately, he couldn't beat anyone else.

Brooklyn started the season with four catchers, holding on to just two of them after reaching the cutdown date in May. Lew McCarty, who could double at first base when an injury took Jake Daubert out of the lineup, was the better hitter. But Otto "Moon" Miller was Robinson's favorite. He played the game the way Robbie had with the Orioles. Winning, not personal statistics, counted with Miller. He would take risks when they were worth taking without worrying about the way they affected his personal record.

There was one insult that would enrage the round-faced Miller. He hated to be called "Moonie" as much as John McGraw loathed being called "Muggsy." One summer evening Miller went to Coney Island and stationed himself at the bar in Feltman's Restaurant,

TRANSCENDENTAL GRAPHICS

Nap Rucker had been one of the premier lefthanders in baseball,
but was on the downhill slide when Robinson took over the Dodgers.

world famous for frankfurters before Nathan Werkheimer called them hot dogs and undercut the price to a nickel. Among the semipro teams playing in small ballparks around Brooklyn were the Kensingtons, named for a Flatbush neighborhood. Their third baseman was Eddie Mooney. While Miller was drinking his beer at the bar, the Kensingtons were gathering for a team party at tables in the rear of the restaurant. As each player arrived, he was greeted and called over to join the team. When the doors swung wide and Eddie Mooney bounded in, his teammates hailed him. "Hey, Mooney," they shouted across the restaurant.

The big Brooklyn catcher at the bar bristled. He slammed down his stein of beer and strode menacingly back to the Kensingtons' party. "Who you calling Moonie?" he demanded. Placatingly, they soothed his injured feelings by introducing their teammate. The catcher was persuaded that the similarity of Mooney and Moonie was accidental and no insult was intended. He bought the team a round of drinks. The story survives because the Kensingtons' right fielder was John Kavanagh, whose son Jack writes baseball histories.

Brooklyn's fan loyalties in 1914 were divided between the National League team in Ebbets Field and the newcomers, the Tip Tops, in Washington Park. Robert B. Ward had brought in the unrelated John Montgomery Ward to run the operation. Bill Bradley, formerly a star third baseman with Cleveland, was the field manager. Monty Ward was a dominant figure in baseball. He had managed Brooklyn teams in the Players' League, which he helped to create in 1890, and in the National League in 1891 and 1892. Off the field, he was a lawyer, earning a law degree between seasons at Columbia University while starring for the New York Giants. He was one of early baseball's best pitchers before switching to shortstop in mid-career. Stardom at both positions eventually earned him a niche in the Baseball Hall of Fame.

The Tip Tops, like other Federal League teams, had a few good players, some retread ex-major leaguers and—mostly—players from the minors. They had lured Tom Seaton away from the Philadelphia Phillies, where he had an even better record in 1913 than Grover Cleveland Alexander. Phillies owner Horace Fogel refused to pay the salary Seaton expected for winning 27 games and let him go to the Feds. In 1914, pitching for Brooklyn's Tip Tops, he won 25 games.

To a certain degree, competition for fans between the two Brooklyn teams became a price war. Fans could go to games at Washington Park for half what they paid at Ebbets Field. Ebbets claimed his games were twice the value as those of the Federal League.

Robinson got his new team off to an encouraging start, winning five of the first seven games. He delighted the Brooklyn fans by beating the Giants and Matty behind a Zack Wheat home run at the Polo Grounds. Unfortunately, the fast start tailed off behind ineffective pitching and the weakness at shortstop.

Charlie Ebbets wanted the world to know he was not discouraged. On June 16, after the team had dropped to last place, Ebbets again let his bankroll express his confidence. He signed Wilbert Robinson

Jeff Pfeffer (left), not to be confused with his big brother, the other *Jeff Pfeffer, was Robinson's first big winner. He won 113 games for Brooklyn. Otto Miller (right) was a hard-nosed catcher and Robinson's kind of player. He remained a favorite for years. Just don't call him "Moonie."*

to a new three-year contract. The next day Brooklyn won a doubleheader from Philadelphia with 10,000 reassured fans on hand. Elmer "Shook" Brown pitched the only complete game of his career for Brooklyn to beat Grover Cleveland Alexander, 10-4.

After he had been given his new contract, Robinson led his team back into the pennant fight. Brooklyn beat Boston in a Fourth of July doubleheader, pushing the Braves deeper into last place with a 26-40 record. Brooklyn was fifth at 31-33. The Giants were far ahead in first place at 40-24, but that year the traditional belief that the team leading on Independence Day would win the pennant did not hold up. The rocketing rise of the Braves to a pennant in the second half of the 1914 season is a baseball legend. Brooklyn climbed with them for a while but fell back when injuries and a lack of adequate reserves revealed a weakness of depth that Ebbets had not covered.

In the July 4 doubleheader, captain Jake Daubert was injured scoring the second game's winning run. Jake had stolen second base, and when catcher Hank Gowdy's throw went wildly into the outfield he set out for third base and never slowed down. The relay had him beaten but he dove head first for the plate, hitting his head on Gowdy's shinguard. Daubert was unconscious for several minutes and out of the lineup for a week. When he got back into action, his play was below par.

Shortstop was the Achilles heel of the Dodgers lineup. O'Mara was flashy but wasn't hitting. When he brooded about it his glove work also went downhill. When he broke his leg in August, his various replacements did nothing to improve the porous condition of the left side of the infield. On the right side the reliable George Cutshaw and Daubert, when he was healthy, were towers of strength. Still, they could not offset the weaknesses across the diamond.

Jack Dalton, who had failed with Brooklyn earlier, had a fine season. He battled Daubert for the batting title, eventually finishing third at .319 while Jake won his second title at .329. Zack Wheat hit .319 and Casey Stengel, who had lagged behind in the early season, closed strongly to hit .315 and put four Brooklyn batters, including the complete outfield, among the league's top five hitters.

Dalton was slowed by a strained tendon late in the season. To replace him, Ebbets brought up a player from Newark, Hy Myers, who would become a Brooklyn stalwart for many years. In 1915, Dalton jumped to the Federal League for a three-year contract at $8,000, plus a $4,000 bonus. Charlie Ebbets never regretted letting Dalton go. At the end of the season he signed Myers to a two-year contract. Brooklyn was assembling a future pennant winner.

9.

THE TRUE GRAPEFRUIT STORY

Robinson's fortunes, like any other manager's, were tied to those of his team's owner. Ebbets put the best players he could afford at his manager's disposal, but his finances were based entirely on his team's success. He had no outside fortune to fall back on. In 1915, the Tip Tops loomed as an economic hazard. Ward used his bankroll to build a better attraction than the Dodgers. He added the outlaw league's most colorful star, Benny Kauff, to his team. Kauff had led the Feds in batting in 1914 with a .370 mark, and his Indianapolis team had won the pennant. Despite this, the franchise lost money and was shifted to Newark for 1915. Ebbets was doubly outraged. Not only did his direct rival bring in a star attraction, the move of a Federal League club to Newark forced the minor league team in which he had an interest to move out.

The Newark Feds had an even better player than Kauff in future Hall of Famer Edd Roush, and they added further to Ebbets' woes by luring Ed Reulbach away from Brooklyn. The veteran won twenty games for a second division Newark team in 1915.

At Brooklyn's spring training site in Daytona, Florida, cloudy skies cleared often enough to permit passenger-carrying flights by a famous aviatrix, Ruth Law, a slender brunette who photographed alluringly in the skin-tight airman's britches she wore. The manly athletes gathered in the Brooklyn training camp were eager to climb into her biplane and soar above the beaches below. Aviation was a fledgling activity and its pioneer pilots were a novelty. They supported themselves by taking up paying passengers for an aerial view of the landscape. To bring more attention to their flights, these pilots sometimes dropped baseballs to be caught below. It was a county fairgrounds stunt. Catching balls from heights was on the public's mind in those days. In 1908 Senators catcher Gabby Street had gained fame by catching a baseball dropped 504 feet from the observatory atop the Washington Monument. It had been done before, in 1894, by Pop Schriver, when visiting with Cap Anson's Chicago White Stockings. Another Chicago catcher, Billy Sullivan, had duplicated Street's catch in fewer tries in 1910.

Ruth Law had already dropped golf balls over the ocean beaches for the finders to redeem for greens fees at the Daytona golf course. Publicity-minded Charlie Ebbets, fifty-five years old, offered to "throw out the first ball" of the spring training season by dropping it from Ruth Law's plane. Whether he had second thoughts or was grounded because the team trainer, Fred Kelly, warned that a man of Ebbets' age and Epicurean lifestyle might not survive at the elevated altitude, the plans were changed.

With Street's catch as a challenge, it was proposed to set a new record. Ruth Law could fly higher than the Washington Monument, but could a ball rocketing down from a greater height be caught? The players argued about it but none of them offered to try. Robbie scoffed at the idea that the stunt was at all difficult. "I could do it myself," boasted the old Oriole. The players and reporters cheered him on and Ruth Law was contacted. She agreed to drop a ball to the practice field from well above 504 feet the next day.

The event has had many tellings, and while the conclusion is always the same, the culprits supposedly involved have been assigned roles they did not play. Casey Stengel, because of his penchant for fun-making stunts, has been put in the plane to make the drop. In some tellings, he only suggested substituting a grapefruit for the baseball and sent Fred Kelly, the team's trainer, aloft with one.

In fact, neither Kelly nor Stengel was in the plane. Ruth Law flew alone. No culprit on the Dodgers planted the grapefruit. In any event, three months short of his fifty-third birthday, Robinson buckled on a chest protector and borrowed a mitt. He peered up at the circling plane and caught sight of a falling object. Just as he had once set himself under pop foul balls for the old Orioles, Robbie positioned himself to make the catch. The grapefruit landed with a splat in his mitt and exploded. The impact knocked him to the ground and the grapefruit drenched him with warm juice.

"Help me, lads, I'm covered with my own blood," he pleaded, his eyes clenched shut. The players laughed uproariously. When he realized what had happened, Robbie gruffly toweled himself off and ordered the players back to their training drills. Later, of course, Robinson accepted the joke with his typical geniality. However, the team had a new trainer the next season when Doc Hart replaced the fun-loving Kelly. Robbie probably suspected Stengel and Kelly—the camp cutups—of complicity. He never knew the real story.

The true account of the grapefruit drop was obtained by sportswriter Harold Rosenthal in 1957. Mrs. Ruth Law Oliver was visiting New York City from her home in San Francisco. In an interview, she confessed that she was the culprit who replaced the baseball with a grapefruit. She explained she had not intended it to be a prank. It became an expedient solution when she realized she had left the baseball back in her hotel room. It was too late to go back so she took a small grapefruit from the lunch of one of her ground crew and took off. She flew over the ballpark where the Dodgers waited in a circle surrounding their manager. She took aim and let the grapefruit drop.

Crediting the grapefruit stunt to Casey Stengel was a matter of retrospective type casting. Actually, 1915 was a sad season for Casey. He arrived in camp weighing twenty pounds less than his stocky frame usually carried. He was gaunt and claimed he had nearly succumbed to typhoid fever during the winter.

Robert Creamer in his biography of Stengel presents a strong case, citing the veteran baseball historian Fred Lieb as a source, that Stengel's woes were from venereal disease. A bachelor, Casey led an active social life. Creamer's book also recounts a morose Stengel contemplating drowning himself. It took the whole season for Casey to regain his health and form. Robinson's characteristic patience and sympathetic way with troubled players gave Stengel the chance to rehabilitate himself. However, it was a wasted year for the outfielder. He didn't play in spring training, or appear at Ebbets Field until he pinch hit for Nap Rucker in a final tune-up game, and he was below par until the last month of the season.

With Reulbach gone to the Feds and Rucker near the end of the trail, Robinson was happy to acquire another former ace who might yet have winning games in his aged arm. Jack Coombs, who had won seventy games in three seasons, 1910-12, for Connie Mack's Athletics, was cut loose as part of Mack's customary payroll-cutting reaction to the challenge of the Federal League. Robinson preferred depth on a staff, and found it in a mixture of veterans and newcomers. The most promising of the rookies were Wheezer Dell, whose big frame measured up to the manager's idea of how a pitcher should be built, and Sherry Smith, a large-sized lefthanded prospect.

Robinson played a set lineup of carryovers, with Hy Myers now in center field. Stengel was in and out of the lineup with the veteran John Hummell responding well as his replacement. Zack Wheat was bothered by a spring cold, as was captain Jake Daubert. The star first baseman was out of the lineup in the early weeks of the season, but led the team in hitting when he returned. Wheat's batting average fell from its previous highs, although he still hit for power and drove in runs . Zack's defense was so great that Robbie would have kept him in the lineup for that alone.

An infield of Daubert, Cutshaw, Getz, and O'Mara lacked excellence only at shortstop. Gee Gee Getz handled third base more than adequately and was an effective hitter. Robinson always said that O'Mara's hands were too small, but he had no one better than the skinny redhead. O'Mara would again take himself out of the lineup with a broken leg late in the season. Ivy Olson, whose erratic form would continue to plague the team, replaced him.

The 1915 Dodgers began slowly. Their best pitcher, Jeff Pfeffer,

Zack (or Zach) Wheat, one of the great Dodgers of all time, was reliably superb year after year. An outstanding outfielder with a great arm, he was also the complete hitter, leading the league in the shortened season of 1918.

was hammered in the opener at the Polo Grounds as Jeff Tesreau, Robinson's former protégé, coasted to a 16-3 win. The next day, Giants fans lorded it over the bumpkins from Brooklyn, particularly when Rube Marquard, Robbie's first pitching project with the Giants, tossed an ingrate's no-hitter, beating Brooklyn, 2-0.

There was momentary hope that a savior had emerged from among the rookie pitchers. Texan Whitey Appleton won his major league debut, 5-3, thanks to a Wheat home run. He won only three more games while losing ten. Raleigh Aitchison, whose specialty had been beating Boston, lost the first time he met them. In 1915 he couldn't beat anyone, ending his major league career with a final 0-4 record.

Brooklyn was in last place at 1-6 before the schedule brought them home for the opening game at Ebbets field. Although Rucker was routed by the Giants, Dell got a 6-4 win in relief over Marquard. The Phillies were off to a pennant-winning season, with Grover Cleveland Alexander on his way to the first of three successive thirty-win seasons. They won their first eight games. The rest of the league could never catch up.

As Brooklyn settled into the second division Robinson made a risky move. He bought pitcher Phil Douglas from the Reds on June 13, hoping he could reform this brilliant pitcher whose known fondness for drink preceded him like an alcoholic's breath. For Brooklyn he was at times dominant. Called "Shufflin' Phil" for his plowboy's gait, he pitched a sixteen-inning scoreless tie against Boston, allowing only one hit in the first nine innings and four in all. He would pitch one or two great games and then be batted out of the box in his next start. With Brooklyn, Douglas was 5 and 5 before Robbie gave up on him and sold him to the Cubs on September 9. Douglas staggered from one team to another. He finally ran out of opportunities when he was banned from baseball in 1922 for pathetically trying to bribe a player on another team.

Self-inflicted misfortune plagued the Robins. Rookie Appleton fell for an old ruse and lost a game in St. Louis. The wily Cardinal manager, Miller Huggins, coaching at third base with the bases filled, demanded that the rookie toss him the ball so he could

Robbie, in Brooklyn's distinctive windowpane uniform shakes hands with Yankees manager Wild Bill Donovan the year after the legendary "grapefruit" incident.

prove Appleton was doctoring it. When Whitey indignantly threw the ball to Huggins, the manager sidestepped. The ball rolled to the stands and the winning run scored.

On August 9, in a game against the Chicago Cubs, Brooklyn's second baseman George Cutshaw rapped out six safe hits. Records were not then computerized and at the fingertips of baseball reporters. The scribes of the day assumed they had witnessed a unique feat and wrote about it. When comment about Cutshaw's one-game outburst ignored Robinson's own seven-hit game back on June 10, 1892, the nationally syndicated Damon Runyon came to the rescue. He printed the box score of Robbie's earlier feat and, in the same column, described the Brooklyn manager as a person of special merit. "He's everybody's Uncle Wilbert," Runyon wrote, praising Robinson for his jovial personality as well as his baseball skills.

A side issue in baseball—whether fans could keep balls hit into the stands—took another turn in 1915. Naturally, owner Ebbets wanted the balls back, but Robinson had a more subtle view of the issue. Claiming that Jack Coombs had been deprived of a win in Boston by fans keeping balls, he urged Dodger fans to be selective, just as they were in Beantown. The locals there, he claimed, kept only balls that had been battered and scuffed when the local team was at bat. This forced the umpires to put a clean ball into the game to the advantage of Boston's batters. Robbie urged Brooklyn's fans to do the same. "Throw back the scuffed balls if our team is in the field," he counseled, "and give our pitchers an edge." To Ebbets' chagrin, Brooklyn fans were impartial in their greed. They kept every ball they could get their hands on and battled ushers and park police to keep them.

As the season moved along, Robinson spotted two more veterans who seemed to have passed their prime. Both became August acquisitions. Larry Cheney had been a 20-game winner the previous three seasons for the Chicago Cubs. In 1915 he appeared to have lost the zip off his fastball and his curve didn't break as it once had. He lost two games for Brooklyn but responded to Robbie's touch the next year with eighteen victories.

The other veteran was Marquard, whose early season no-hitter for the Giants had been followed by a string of failures. Finally, McGraw put Rube on waivers and Robinson claimed him. It was like a father welcoming his prodigal son's return. Robbie told the papers that Rube was ill and kept him out of action for several weeks. He was waiting for the Giants to make their next visit to Ebbets Field. He planned to show up McGraw's judgment by springing a primed Marquard on him. Robinson ordered Marquard to warm up under the grandstand and not appear on the field until the umpires yelled, "Play ball." Marquard carried out his orders, trotted on the field from under the stands and went ten innings to shut out his old team, 1-0.

"Robbie was always looking to put something over on McGraw," Marquard told reporters after Robinson died. "He did that day and I still remember how he grabbed his left cuff with his right hand and laughed up his sleeve right in front of old John after the game." Marquard was only 2-2 the rest of the season as the Robins bobbed up to third place with a strong finish. He, like Cheney, would repay Robinson's faith in him in the next season.

Had Phil Douglas been sober enough often enough, had Cheney and Marquard been obtained sooner to join fifteen-game winner Coombs, Robinson might have won his first flag in 1915. As it was, with a glaring weakness at shortstop, an outfield that fell far below the level of the 1914 trio, and a patchwork pitching staff, his club scrapped its way to a third-place finish, ten games behind the Phillies. The hated Giants were dead last.

Charlie Ebbets had weathered the Federal League. It collapsed after 1915, leaving Brooklyn with key players already under contract for the coming season. Because they had signed lucrative multiyear contracts, they would report happy, knowing they were better paid than most of their colleagues. Not for the last time, the hot stove league sizzled in anticipation in Brooklyn's saloons and political clubhouses. Everyone optimistically waited for next year.

10.

ROBBIE'S FIRST WINNER

When the coastal steamer Arapahoe sailed from New York harbor to carry Brooklyn ballplayers to their 1916 Florida spring training camp, Robinson was aboard with his son, Wilbert Robinson Jr.. They set off on the high seas with high hopes. It was a holiday excursion. The sinking of the British liner Lusitania by German U-Boats in the North Atlantic the previous May was no cause for alarm. America was neutral. Woodrow Wilson would be reelected in 1916 on the slogan, "He kept us out of war." It was safe enough to hug the East Coast shoreline, although ocean travelers could bring their own life jackets aboard if they wished. The Arapahoe's lights blazed while passengers danced and partied the nights away. Americans were only distantly concerned with the Great War. Winning a pennant and the World Series were the conquests that concerned most Americans.

Brooklyn fans were optimistic. Robbie had brought his team home third with a late-season surge the year before. Charlie Ebbets' strategy of signing his core players to multiyear contracts kept his team intact. The team that assembled at Daytona Beach was much the same as the one that had finished fast in 1915. Robinson would have preferred a Texas training site like the Giants', but Ebbets shied away from a place where the bandit Pancho Villa was raiding American towns across the border.

Both Rube Marquard and Larry Cheney quickly flashed their old form at their first Brooklyn training camp. Marquard was helped by another Giant émigré, his former batterymate, Chief Meyers. A Dartmouth-educated Cahuilla Indian from the West Coast, Meyers would mostly catch Marquard. Matching the former Giant teammates fitted Robinson's idea to pair each pitcher with a catcher who worked well with him.

Jeff Pfeffer could be counted on to pitch every fourth day, regardless of the opposition. Jack Coombs promised another season of successful spot starting. The kind of loose rotation Robbie preferred was strung together by working in Sherry Smith and Wheezer Dell. Nap Rucker continued to be plagued by a sore arm and would be of little use, except in helping to develop the left-handed Sherry Smith. The six starters—Pfeffer, Coombs, Marquard, Cheney, Smith, and Dell—all were built to Robinson's ideal specifications. They were big men, all six feet or taller, and each weighing 200 pounds or more.

There was nothing Robinson liked more than getting the best of John McGraw, and he delighted in the Brooklyn success of former Giants Rube Marquard (left) and battery mate Chief Meyers.

Despite threats to players who had jumped to the Federal League that they would never be allowed back, major league clubs immediately scrambled for the best of them. The New York Giants signed Benny Kauff, dubbed "the Ty Cobb of the Federal League." A good hitter, a speedy baserunner, and a fine fielder and thrower, Kauff had other problems. His unsavory associations with criminals branded him as untrustworthy. McGraw also nabbed future Hall of Famers Edd Roush and Bill McKechnie from Newark.

Actually, there had been very few genuine major league prospects on the rosters of the Federal League teams. Some big name stars, such as Brooklyn's Reulbach, had too little left to draw offers. Looking over the lot, Ebbets and Robinson picked up third baseman Mike Mowrey. The disbanded league had no first-class shortstops to offer. Joe Tinker, who only a few years earlier had seemed the answer before he jumped to the new league, had retired as an active player while managing the Chicago Whales.

In 1916 shortstop would be divided between Ollie O'Mara and Ivy Olson. Neither hit a major leaguer's average, but Olson had some power and a knack for getting a hit in the clutch. Unfortunately, he also had the knack of making an error in the clutch. Robinson would juggle his shortstops without solving the problem until O'Mara broke his leg in August. Olson became the everyday shortstop.

All during the 1916 season, Ebbets eyed star shortstop Buck Herzog, who was managing the Cincinnati Reds. Herzog had helped the Giants win pennants in 1911, '12 and '13, when Robbie was a Giant coach. Ebbets wanted to see if their chemistry would work in Brooklyn. Unfortunately, John McGraw intervened.

Following his three pennants and three World Series failures, McGraw had terminated both his best friend, Wilbert Robinson, and his worst enemy, Buck Herzog. The Giants had been without a pennant since. The fiery shortstop was a player McGraw couldn't stand to have on his team, but he couldn't seem to win without him. He shipped Mathewson, Roush, and McKechnie to Cincinnati for the shortstop he despised. The Dodgers were forced to keep Ivy Olson in their lineup.

Brooklyn did add Jimmy Johnston, a first-class ballplayer, to the squad. Johnston came up as an outfielder but was versatile enough to play all infield positions. Strangely, Robinson never tried him at shortstop. He was a good hitter with extra base power. When Hy Myers was injured during the 1916 season, Johnston plugged the hole, flanked by the team's outfield stars, Zack Wheat and Casey Stengel.

Captain Jake Daubert, still enjoying the salary and long-term contract he had extracted from Ebbets under the threat of jumping to the Federal League, was beginning to slow in the field, and Johnston often filled in at first base. Late in the season Robbie picked up another former New York Giant, first baseman Fred Merkle. Never to shed the undeserved nickname "Bonehead" for a rookie's mistake in a crucial game in 1908, Merkle joined the other former Giants on Robinson's team.

The infield was completed by George Cutshaw, still as good as any second baseman in the league, and Mowrey, the solid performer at third.

The National League pennant race would be marked by record-setting winning and losing streaks. The New York Giants contributed the most bizarre of these, in consecutive games both won and lost. Philadelphia, the defending National League champions, couldn't pull away from the pack despite another sensational season by Grover Cleveland Alexander. Ol' Pete won a career high thirty-three games. Sixteen of these were shutouts, half of them pitched in Baker Bowl, Philadelphia's bandbox home park. The Boston Braves, the dramatic 1914 champions, were in the running all season. However, Wilbert Robinson got his team out of the gate in front of the pack. Like a well-rated thoroughbred on a short lead, the Robins led into the stretch and turned for home in a ding-dong pennant drive. Once caught and once headed, they came on again like a true champion.

It was an exhausting season. The streaks of the Giants added pyrotechnics to the pennant race. They were up and down the league standings, leading at times and tail-enders at others. Brooklyn started well with Robinson craftily selecting his pitchers, although Pfeffer started every fourth day. By May any hope that Rucker would return to form was gone, but Robbie had a pitching staff that was strong and long, and he was a master at sending his starters to the mound in the right situation for each of them to win.

The Giants drew the attention of baseball fans. McGraw, last in 1915, rebuilt his team halfway through the 1916 season. The Giants had begun promisingly but McGraw sensed they were playing over their heads. They soon lapsed into a swoon and hit bottom. A disgusted McGraw banned wives, including his own Blanche, from road trips as his team left on a long swing through the league's western cities. The Giants did an about-face and won seventeen straight games, nineteen of twenty-one in all. Then they returned home to their wives and the expected benefit of playing before local fans. Only half a game behind Robinson's first-place Dodgers, the Giants then lost ten of fifteen games at the Polo Grounds.

In midseason McGraw made his move to reconstruct this erratic team, getting Herzog back and building around him. Once again road success resulted in a winning streak, this time of twenty-six straight victories—still the record. However, it came too late. The Giants ran out of both steam and time in the last week of the season. Despite their great surge, they did not threaten Brooklyn and Philadelphia, who were battling for the pennant. After a Friday game in Brooklyn was rained out on September 29, the Phillies actually got into first place, winning the makeup game played the next day on a Saturday morning.

Charlie Ebbets saw the opportunity to sell out his ballpark twice. For the morning game, he accepted as rainchecks tickets from the previous day's cancellation. He sold separate tickets to the afternoon game. The fans were outraged. They had expected a bargain double bill. Ebbets did not give away such bargains. He squeezed every dollar he could out of his franchise. When the team was on the road he leased the park for any purpose. At night, motion pictures were shown in front of the grandstand. At the National League's annual meeting that winter, Ebbets campaigned to limit the number of 50-cent seats a club could sell. Ebbets Field, with 21,000 seats, had only 2,000 bleacher seats at half a buck.

Ebbets wanted other cities to sell fewer cheap seats when the Dodgers came to town. This, he reasoned, would create a larger visitor's share of the gate receipts. The idea did not appeal to the other owners.

The pennant race hung on the set of games between the Phillies and Dodgers. Eppa Rixey beat Pfeffer, 7-2, in the morning game. The Phillies took first place while Ebbets emptied the ball park and refilled it with new ticket holders. At this point Philadelphia was 89-57 and Brooklyn 90-59, a half-game and six percentage points behind.

With Alexander to work the afternoon game for the Phillies, Brooklyn could have folded. However, Robinson had Marquard primed to start. During his seasons with the Giants, Marquard, not Christy Mathewson, had been McGraw's choice to face Alexander. Rube had held his own against Alex and would again this time. Both teams scored in the opening inning and then goose eggs were hung on the scoreboard. Then Brooklyn scored a run in the fifth inning, another in the sixth, and one more in the seventh. With Alex gone for a pinch hitter, Brooklyn added two more runs on a Stengel home run for a final score of 6-1. Rube Marquard had held the Phillies scoreless on three hits over the last eight innings.

That same day the Giants' twenty-six-game winning streak came to an end in Boston. Brooklyn fans hoped this signaled the loss of momentum for the Giants. They would close the season with three games at Ebbets Field. They couldn't finish first themselves, but they could keep the Dodgers from doing so. McGraw would particularly enjoy yanking the pennant from Robinson's grasp.

No games involving the contenders were played on Sunday. Blue laws prohibiting professional play on the Sabbath kept the teams idle. The residents of the Borough of Churches flocked to houses of worship to pray for a Brooklyn pennant. On Monday, Jack Coombs shut out the Giants while the Phillies split a doubleheader in Boston. Brooklyn led by a full game. Philadelphia would end the season with another doubleheader in Boston. Brooklyn had two more games with the Giants. A Brooklyn victory, coupled with a Philadelphia loss, would mean that the 1916 pennant flew over

Ebbets Field. John McGraw vowed it wouldn't happen. Actually, it was not first place that McGraw was focused on, but third, at that time the lowest finish that would get a team a share of World Series money. Word came later that McGraw had bet heavily on the Giants to finish third. The Braves, in that spot, would be dislodged if the Phillies beat them. Full of confidence, McGraw sent his Giants into the final doubleheader. He expected to knock the Robins off their perch.

It did not work out the way John McGraw intended.

In Boston, the Braves won the first game and were leading the Phillies in the second. In Brooklyn, the Giants were leading in the first game, 4-1, when they fell apart. The Dodgers rallied, but some of their base hits were ground balls that were only waved at by Giants infielders. Fly balls that seemed catchable dropped safely. The Dodgers won, 7-5, but McGraw was not around to see the end. He had stormed out of his dugout and left the ballpark. Furiously he shouted, "You bunch of quitters," at his players. He refused to simmer down, and gave a press interview in which he stopped barely short of accusing his players of throwing the game.

The reporters had a field day. The consensus was that the Giants had eased up so their former buddies, Marquard, Meyers and Merkle, now wearing Brooklyn's checkered uniforms, could get World Series shares. And, of course, there was no love lost between the fiery McGraw and many of his players. The Giants did, however, have a gift they had planned to present to their manager after the final game. It was a leather-bound set of Shakespeare's works in twenty-six volumes, symbolizing the twenty-six-game winning streak. The books eventually were sent to McGraw's apartment, but ignoring the coming World Series, McGraw and Blanche had already left for their home in Baltimore, where Mac spent his days at the Laurel racetrack.

The Dodgers celebrated their pennant. When Zack Wheat, whose Indian stoicism rarely allowed a show of emotion, caught a fly ball for the final out, he exuberantly threw it to the fans and raced for the clubhouse where the Dodgers were congratulating Robbie, who stood on a bench and thanked his players. They snake-danced around the locker room but thought better of trying to boost the rotund Robinson to their shoulders.

Some of the Giants came by to offer congratulations, particularly to their former coach and teammates. They were embarrassed by McGraw's outburst, although no one knew yet of the press conference where he had made his feelings public. Robbie, when he did learn of McGraw's charges, was outraged. According to Harold Seymour's classic history, *Baseball: The Golden Age*, he complained, "He piddled on my pennant." It is nicely alliterative, but the scholarly Dr. Seymour has undoubtedly softened Robinson's language. Jolly Uncle Robbie was truly pissed off.

11.

THE ROBINS FOLD THEIR WINGS IN BOSTON

A parade of eighteen touring cars, with Wilbert Robinson and Charlie Ebbets leading the way, left Ebbets Field and traveled down Flatbush Avenue. Sidewalk spectators cheered the cavalcade as it passed and headed over the Brooklyn Bridge into the alien territory of Manhattan. The cars carrying the Brooklyn Dodgers drove uptown to the Grand Central Station. There, 5,000 cheering fans sent the new National League champions on to Boston where the defending World Champion Red Sox awaited them. It was a familiar trip. Brooklyn regularly visited Boston during the National League season. Even the ball park would be familiar. The Red Sox used the newer and larger Braves Field for their World Series games, as they had the year before when they beat the Phillies.

In contrast to the merry thousands who had sent the team on its way, there were only a few hundred Brooklyn fans in the stands for the opening game of the Series. Uncle Robbie had left tickets for his friends and former neighbors from nearby Hudson, but these supporters were drowned out by the noisy contingent of Red Sox boosters who called themselves the "Royal Rooters." Their marching band serenaded with the jaunty music hall number, "Tessie," and played it over and over. Mayor "Honey Fitz" Fitzgerald, JFK's grandfather, threw out the first ball.

The Red Sox were so strong that even the loss of Tris Speaker to Cleveland after the previous season had made little impact.

Defense made the Red Sox tick. Tillie Walker could not hit like Speaker, but he was a fine center fielder. Like Speaker, he played close behind the infield and was phenomenal at going back to pull down long flies. Walker was flanked by Duffy Lewis in left and Harry Hooper in right. There was no better outfield in baseball.

The infield lacked star-quality players, but Dick Hoblitzell at first, Hal Janvrin at second, Everett Scott at short, and Larry Gardner at third played airtight ball and all were better than average hitters. Manager Bill Carrigan, one of the era's top backstops, shared the catching duties with Hick Cady and Sam Agnew.

Carrigan's pitching staff, like Robinson's, was deep with starting pitchers: Ernie Shore, Carl Mays, Dutch Leonard, Rube Foster, and the youthful Babe Ruth. The Babe was the best lefty in the league with twenty-three wins, nine of them shutouts, and a 1.75 ERA. The two managers would match their starters in the World Series. Robbie made the first call. Instead of starting twenty-five-game winner Jeff Pfeffer, he used the rejuvenated Rube Marquard (13-6). He believed Boston was more vulnerable to lefthanders. Marquard had long experience in World Series play and Robinson, as a Giants coach, had seen Rube beat the Red Sox twice in the 1912 World Series. For good measure, Chief Meyers, who caught Marquard's victories in 1912, would be behind the plate. The Chief and the other Dodgers now wore Brooklyn's novel checkerboard design uniform. In black-and-white photos the thin lines have been mistaken as dark blue. Only the vertical lines were blue. The horizontal lines were crimson. Charlie Ebbets had wanted a patriotic red, white, and blue effect.

Carrigan started 6-foot-4, 215-pound Ernie Shore (16-10), who had beaten the Phillies twice in the 1915 World Series. The Sox manager hoped for a repeat performance.

Both Shore and Marquard were in less than top form through six innings ,but the game was close. Boston scored first, in the third inning, when Hoblitzell's two-out triple was followed by Lewis's double. Meyers picked Lewis off second to end the inning.

Casey Stengel led off the fourth inning with a single and scored on Zack Wheat's triple. Then George Cutshaw looped a short fly ball to right field. Wheat started for home, but when Hooper made a diving catch, he went back, tagged up at third, and dashed for the plate. Hooper, possessor of one of baseball's storied arms, gunned him down.

Boston regained the lead in the fifth, scoring twice. A run in the seventh and another in the ninth increased their lead to 6-1, and it appeared the Dodgers were dead. Not quite. Jake Daubert walked to open the top of the ninth. Stengel singled. Daubert, who had stopped at second base, was forced out at third when Wheat hit back to the box. The tiring Shore walked Cutshaw to load the bases. Janvrin booted Mike Mowrey's ground ball far enough for two runs to score. When Ivy Olson beat out a grounder to short, the bases were loaded again. Meyers popped out to first. Fred Merkle, hitting for Pfeffer, who had pitched the eighth in relief of Marquard, walked, forcing in the third run, leaving Brooklyn two runs behind and the bases loaded.

Carrigan brought Carl Mays in to pitch. Hy Myers beat out a ground ball single to second and the Robins were only one run behind, still with the bases loaded. Daubert, whose walk had opened the ninth inning, came to bat again. Another walk would tie the game. A base hit could put Brooklyn in front. Daubert shot a grounder deep into the hole between second and third. Everett Scott speared it and fired across the diamond to nip him. The game was over and Boston led in the Series.

Still believing a lefthander could beat the Red Sox, Robinson again held Jeff Pfeffer out and started Sherry Smith in the second game. Boston started Babe Ruth. Robbie benched lefthanded hitting Casey Stengel, despite his two hits and two runs scored in the opener. Jimmy Johnston, his replacement, went hitless in five at bats. In all, Brooklyn could manage only six hits and a lone run in fourteen innings.

After Brooklyn scored a first-inning run on Hy Myers' inside-the-park homer, Ruth posted thirteen consecutive scoreless innings. Smith countered with his own string of goose eggs after Boston scored a run in the fifth when Scott tripled and came home on Ruth's infield ground out. After that the two lefties were in total control.

Boston threatened in the ninth inning, but Wheat's perfect throw to the plate nailed Hal Janvrin trying to score on Hoblitzell's fly out.

The game drew a record 47,373 spectators, who got their money's worth as the two lefthanders dueled into the deepening twilight. Boston sent their fans home happy by scoring the deciding run in the bottom of the fourteenth inning. Hoblitzell drew his fourth walk of the game and was sacrificed to second. The speedier Mike McNally ran for him and scored when Del Gainer, pinch-hitting for Larry Gardner, singled him home.

Ruth's thirteen scoreless innings became part of his record 29-2/3 consecutive scoreless World Series innings which stretched into the 1918 Series. This record stood for over forty years, until it was broken by the Yankees' Whitey Ford in 1962. After he retired, Ruth often claimed this streak was, of all his records, the one he was proudest of.

Despite the two one-run losses in Boston, Robinson insisted that his boys would turn things around when the Series shifted to Ebbets Field. After record crowds in Boston, the 21,087 who turned out in Brooklyn sounds disappointing, but that was all the seats there were. Thousands milled around in the famed Rotunda looking for tickets. Once again, Robbie kept his ace Jeff Pfeffer under wraps. He elected to start the veteran Jack Coombs, who had won three games for the A's in the 1910 World Series and another in 1911. Coombs had never lost a World Series game and his mastery held up through the first five innings. Carl Mays started for Boston and gave up four runs, three of them earned, before being lifted for a pinch hitter in the sixth. The Red Sox scored twice in that frame to narrow the margin to two runs. They closed to within one in the seventh, when Gardner homered over the right field wall. Coombs exited and Jeff Pfeffer entered to slam the door on the Red Sox. He pitched hitless ball, walked none and struck out three to close out the game.

Trailing two games to one, the Dodgers were confident. They could even the Series by winning the next day in Brooklyn, and needed only a split back in Boston to bring the final game back home. The Red Sox, however, had a different scenario in mind.

Robinson came back with Rube Marquard. Bill Carrigan's choice to start was one of his own lefties, Dutch Leonard, an 18-game winner. As he had when Ruth pitched the second game, the Brooklyn manager benched Stengel. He also held Daubert out.

The strategy looked great as the game started and Marquard set down the Red Sox in order, striking out two batters. Jimmy Johnston, playing in Stengel's place, led off for Brooklyn with a triple and Hy Myers singled him home. Fred Merkle, Daubert's replacement, drew a walk. Wheat forced Merkle at second but moved up a base on a wild pitch. The Red Sox appeared to be cracking when Hal Janvrin booted Cutshaw's ground ball, Myers scoring and Wheat going to third. Robinson, trying to capitalize on Boston's shaky start, put on a double steal. The way the old Orioles had designed the play, the runner on third held near the base until the catcher threw to second base. The Red Sox had a strategy of their own. Hal Janvrin cut in front of the bag, took Carrigan's throw, and whipped it to third base to nail Wheat, who had taken his fist step toward home and was trying to scramble back. Mowrey then fanned. The Robins had posted two runs but blew a chance to break the game open.

Fortune reversed itself immediately. Marquard walked Boston's leadoff batter, Hoblitzell, on four pitches. Duffy Lewis doubled off the right field wall, and Larry Gardner's inside-the-park home run cleared the bases to give Boston a 3-2 lead.

Leonard pitched brilliantly after the first inning. Robinson's decision to use righthanded batters produced only a so-so 1-for-4 for Johnston and 1-for-3 for Merkle. Each also contributed an error on defense. Meanwhile, the Red Sox forged ahead, 6-2. Larry Cheney relieved Marquard after a run had scored in the fourth and gave up single runs in the fifth and seventh innings.

Brooklyn fans had to settle for the nostalgic thrill of Nap Rucker's farewell. Wilbert Robinson was a sentimentalist and had kept Rucker on the staff hoping for a suitable final opportunity. This seemed to be it. The sore-armed former ace of the staff stemmed the Red Sox tide too late. He got Gardner and Scott, the first two batters in the eighth, on ground balls, then fanned

Carrigan. After Brooklyn went quietly in the eighth, Rucker returned to the mound for what would be his final inning in baseball. Leonard struck out and Hooper, after reaching second on a single and a bobbled outfield ball by Johnston, was out trying to steal third. Hal Janvrin was called out on strikes. Rucker's great fastball was long gone. His final superb performance had depended on slow curves. After the Dodgers went scoreless in the ninth, the 6-2 loss left the Brooklyn fans nothing positive to talk about except old Nap's two-inning stint. There was plenty of second guessing of Robinson's benching Casey Stengel and Jake Daubert. A dispirited Dodger team headed back to Boston, now trailing three games to one. They would have to win both games to get back to Ebbets Field.

Red Sox fans filled Braves Field, setting an attendance record of 43,620 on Columbus Day. Pfeffer finally got a start. He faced Ernie Shore, winner of the first game. The Red Sox pitcher was even better the second time. Except for a run that scored on a passed ball, he kept Brooklyn in check, giving up only three hits in a 4-1 victory to clinch the World Series. It was Boston's second title in a row.

Wilbert Robinson, already signed for the 1917 season, was rewarded with a $5,000 bonus. The Series had been a disappointment to him, but Charlie Ebbets and most fans realized that he had performed a baseball miracle, bringing Brooklyn a pennant with a team cobbled together from spare parts.

12.

THE COGS OF A CHAMPIONSHIP TEAM SLIP

Robinson spent the winter months at his home in Baltimore, where a room for Wilbert Jr., who had been ill for several years, had been fitted out as a hospital room. Robbie's younger son, Harry, had graduated from Baltimore's Polytechnic High School, where he starred in football, and then entered the construction business. Daughters Hannah and Mary were now in their thirties. Mary had married Frank Gunther of the Baltimore brewing family. Hannah, a semi-invalid with a weak heart that would take her life in 1929, helped her mother care for her half-brother. Mrs. Robinson, now affectionately known to all of Brooklyn as "Ma," would argue strategy and lineups with anyone she met, often exchanging views with fans while Uncle Robbie listened. In the off-season, she was resigned to outdoor sports luring her husband away. A good golfer and an accomplished pool player who had owned his own billiard academy, Robinson divided his time between the needs of the Baltimore family home and the companionship he relished with his hunting and fishing friends.

Even though Brooklyn had lost the World Series and his namesake son was mostly confined to bed, Robinson had pleasant memories of the past season. He had led a lightly-regarded team to a pennant, and the World Series had been closely contested. He was among the highest-paid managers, comfortably signed to a contract for the coming season.

Americans, in the winter of 1916-17, kept a wary eye on the war that raged in Europe even as they enjoyed traditional hot stove league discussions. As pitchers and catchers followed by full squads reported south for spring training, the United States edged toward joining the conflict. On Good Friday, April 6, 1917, America declared war on Germany. At first the war had little impact on baseball. Contracts for the season had been mailed in January; by early April all players were signed. It wasn't until mid-summer that the military draft began to take players from major league teams. Major league baseball began on schedule in 1917 and finished its full 154-game season.

That spring, Charlie Ebbets was about to launch a war of his own with his players. Those multi-year contracts, which had preserved the team but paid Brooklyn players some of the game's highest salaries, had expired after the 1916 season. Ebbets expected salaries would return to their former levels. His players, National League champions, thought otherwise. Contracts calling for substantial reductions were mailed out. Players who expected to be rewarded with increases for their first-place finish mailed them back unsigned.

Casey Stengel, who had been paid $6,000 but was now offered $4,600, sent his contract back with a sarcastic letter suggesting Ebbets had confused him with Red Hanrahan, a clubhouse assistant. Ebbets had never been happy with Stengel's attitude. As a self-made tycoon, he expected deference from his players, and Casey didn't know the meaning of the word.

Ebbets appealed to the fans through the newsmen who covered the Dodgers for Brooklyn's four dailies, the *Eagle*, the *Times*, the *Union*, and the *Standard*. New York's fourteen dailies also covered the Brooklyn team. Ebbets was a generous host, providing a paid winter vacation for those writers assigned to cover spring training games. The news reports filed from spring training were less about the activities of the players on hand than about those who were absent. The team Robinson would lead in an effort to retain the league championship lacked seven of the players who had won it. Zack Wheat, Hy Myers, Jeff Pfeffer, Sherry Smith, Mike Mowrey, and Ollie O'Mara were holdouts along with Stengel. Ebbets' strategies in settling the terms for these players had mixed results.

He dumped Mowrey and O'Mara, selling them to minor league teams. Before the 1917 season ended, they would return to the Brooklyn roster, chastised and still underpaid. Jeff Pfeffer was new at the art of wangling a better salary. He boarded a train at Little Rock to argue his case with Ebbets, who was aboard and headed for Hot Springs. The Dodgers would train there that spring near the Red Sox. Ebbets persuaded Pfeffer on the ride that retaining his 1916 salary level, when everyone else was being cut, was actually an increase. Sherry Smith capitulated to the same argument and came to terms with the team.

However, Ebbets was outmaneuvered by Myers. When the contract failed to reflect the higher esteem in which he held himself, he decided to bluff his way to an increase. He had a few letterheads printed up for the Hy Myers Stock Farm and returned the document unsigned, advising Ebbets that he could ill afford to play baseball for the small salary he was offered, as he owned a prosperous farm at his home in Ohio. Ebbets called his bluff and wired Myers to expect a visit from him to discuss his contract. Myers appealed to his friends and neighbors to lend him their livestock so he could impress his boss. Ebbets fell for the ruse. He believed the impressive array of horses and cows he saw at the Myers homestead belonged to the outfielder. He signed Myers for a boost in pay and hoped to do better when he called on Wheat on his farm in Missouri.

Wheat did not have to round up a display from his neighbors. He had already developed a comfortable farm and turned down an offer for a small raise. Ebbets was outraged. His one-man diplomatic campaign was a failure. He knew from experience that the best strategy to use with a holdout was to get him to report to camp and bargain there. Once a ballplayer was within the sound of bat hitting ball and saw his teammates in action, his resolve would weaken.

But Wheat wouldn't come to camp unsigned. Finally, a group of reporters, hoping to break the logjam and break a story as well, sent a fake telegram to Wheat: "Report at once." It was signed C.H. Ebbets. Thinking that his terms would be met on arrival,

Wheat headed for Hot Springs. Indignantly, Ebbets told him that he had not sent such a telegram. However, as long as Wheat was there, they could talk over the matter. Using much the same logic with Wheat that had worked with Smith and Pfeffer, Ebbets justified the small boost Zack was given by pointing out most of his teammates had been given cuts in salary. Ebbets was within one rebellious player, Casey Stengel, of being able to turn a full team over to Robinson to start the 1917 season.

Again the press played the catalyst. Abe Yager of the Brooklyn *Eagle* sent a telegram to Casey Stengel expressing the team's need for him. He was urged to come down from Kansas City to meet with Robinson and Ebbets and work things out.

Robinson wanted Stengel back. He excused the poor performances in 1915 and part of 1916, citing Casey's ill health. Ebbets, on the other hand, blamed him for it, hinting in his remarks there was nothing to be sympathetic about when a man's social behavior resulted in below-par play. Although he had sent a new contract for even less money to Stengel, Ebbets reluctantly agreed to return to the $4,600 offer. Stengel signed after Ebbets agreed to insert a bonus clause to reward Stengel if his performance reached 1914 levels. Peace, but not harmony, was achieved. The Robins were virtually unchanged from the championship team of the year before. But the team that Ebbets had signed for Robbie to manage looked better on paper than it performed on the field.

The euphoria of a surprise pennant in 1916, followed by a closely contested World Series against a clearly superior Red Sox team, faded as it became clear that the Brooklyn lineup was fundamentally unsound. Robinson had known that it was not likely to become a dynasty. Parts that had held together for one season needed replacement.

The good news for Ebbets was that a long series of exhibition games with their Boston rivals, featuring the wunderkind, Babe Ruth, would draw big crowds as the two clubs played their way north from Hot Springs. The bad news was that these games showed how poorly prepared the Robins were for 1917. When, on opening day, the Robins, with bats militarily shouldered like rifles,

Cool Casey Stengel at home in the Ebbets Field outfield. He was a fine player decades before he became the beloved "old perfesser," but he was also a "Daffy Dodger" years before the term was invented by the press.

trailed Robinson to the center field flagpole to raise the 1916 pennant, they straggled out of step. Instead of being caught in a brisk April breeze, the flag drooped, becalmed. It might as well have been flown at half staff in expectation of the season to come. The Robins plummeted to a seventh-place finish.

Charlie Ebbets finally managed to get around Brooklyn's ban on Sunday baseball. He presented a band concert and an exhibition military drill and announced that all proceeds would benefit wartime charities. On July 1, over 12,000 who attended just happened also to see a regular season ball game. The Robins won, 3-2, beating the Phillies.

Robinson, an avid golfer, applied a philosophy to managerial decisions learned from studying too many putts too long. "Miss 'em quick" was his technique. Brooklyn, fated to lose eighty-one games before their season ended, would lose none faster than the 1-0 defeat by the Giants on August 30. They were off the field at the Polo Grounds in fifty-seven minutes, New York scoring in the bottom of the ninth off Jack Coombs. Losing teams can gain some satisfaction by being spoilers. On October 4, Brooklyn snapped Boston's scoreless inning string at forty, winning 5-1.

The starting pitchers, so deftly spotted by Robinson in 1916, failed to respond to his matchups in 1917. Jeff Pfeffer dropped from 25-10 to 11-15, and no one took up the slack. Cheney went from 18-12 to 8-12. Sherry Smith at least broke even at 12-12 after a 14-12 season the year before. Rube Marquard led the staff with nineteen wins, six more than in 1916, but lost four more. Coombs, often a tough-luck loser, had been 13-8 in 1916 and slipped to 7-11. Given the sorry state of the team, rookie Leon Cadore's 13-13 record and 2.45 ERA were promising. He would become one of Robbie's reliable pitchers in the future.

In 1916 Brooklyn's pitching staff had led the league in ERA at 2.12. In 1917 they ranked next to last at 2.78. Batting went down from a team average of .261 to .247. Only Zack Wheat hit according to form at .312, third in the league. But he was injured almost a third of the season, playing in only ninety-five games with ten more as a pinch hitter.

The war had an indirect influence on Wilbert Robinson's career and reputation in baseball history. The New York Yankees had been bought before the 1915 season by two wealthy men, Jacob Ruppert, a brewery owner, and Tillinghast L'Hommedieu Huston, an engineer. Huston offered his services to the federal government and was commissioned a colonel. He was quickly sent to Europe with the American Expeditionary Force (AEF). Back in New York, Ruppert, also a colonel but an honorary one in a state pseudomilitary organization, wanted to change managers. Huston was agreeable, provided the new manager was his hunting companion, Wilbert Robinson.

It was not an unlikely choice. Despite the poor 1917 season, Robinson was a rising managerial star. He had been a coach for the New York Giants pennant winners in 1911, 1912, and 1913, noted for his ability to get the most out of pitchers. His first two seasons in Brooklyn had demonstrated his ability to build a club. He had sneaked home a pennant winner with the patched-together team in 1916. And he was popular with fans and the press.

Nonetheless, and despite his partner's preference, Ruppert's eye was on St. Louis Cardinals manager Miller Huggins, so scrawny he looked as though the husky Brooklyn manager could have eaten him for breakfast. He was a lawyer and a brilliant ballfield strategist. On October 26, Ruppert signed him, ending the speculation about Robinson.

The two colonels broke over the signing of Huggins. Although the final buyout came in 1923, Ruppert enjoyed the future Yankee triumphs alone in the owners' box. Huston would have one "I told you so" chance, in 1920 when Robbie won another pennant and the Yankees fell short. But 1920 was also the year Ruppert's money secured Babe Ruth for the Yankees. The great Yankee teams that followed insured that Miller Huggins would be remembered. But suppose Colonel Huston had succeeded in putting Robinson in charge of those juggernaut teams? Where would Wilbert Robinson rank among the great all-time managers? Would he have lost pennants that Huggins won? How would he have handled the rambunctious Ruth? We'll never know, and Robinson instead is best remembered for his adventures with a team unimaginably different from the Yankees—the Daffy Dodgers of the Roaring Twenties.

13.

WARTIME BASEBALL

When Wilbert Robinson Jr. succumbed to his long illness on January 6, 1918, his father was devastated. He was given warm support from all quarters: old teammates, rivals of the past and present, his players and, particularly, Charlie Ebbets, all of whom tried to console him. Robinson finally put aside his grief while he busied himself for a return to Hot Springs, Arkansas, for spring training.

Robbie knew his team had to be rebuilt for the future. But by 1918 the full-scale involvement of the United States in the war in Europe had changed the baseball scene. Robinson and Ebbets were limited in what they could do to improve the Dodgers. Trades were made more difficult because players might enlist or be drafted. Nonetheless, in January, Ebbets brought Burleigh Grimes and Al Mamaux from Pittsburgh in a trade for Casey Stengel, whom Ebbets was glad to be rid of, and second baseman George Cutshaw, who appeared to have played himself out. Robbie thought Grimes and Mamaux would win for him.

Mamaux, who had battled with the Pirates over salary withheld when he was suspended, became Brooklyn's first wartime roster casualty when he joined the Army. He turned up once on a furlough during the season to start a single game, which he lost.

Before the team went to spring training, Ebbets learned that Jeff Pfeffer had joined the Navy. Charlie sent him a watch with the team's best wishes, only to have Jeff, sporting the watch, stroll into camp in Hot Springs. His status had been misunderstood, he explained. He had joined the Naval Reserve Auxiliary Force. However, before the team broke camp, Jeff was called to active duty and headed for the Great Lakes Naval Training Station in Chicago. In July, when the Robins were playing the Cubs at Wrigley Field, Pfeffer was given permission by the Navy to pitch for Brooklyn. In old-time form, he pitched a two-hit shutout.

In Brooklyn, Lieutenant Leon Cadore, U.S. Army, on leave after finishing his officer's training, was permitted to pitch while awaiting assignment. He shut out the Cardinals on four hits. Robbie's easy profanity flowed as he wondered at what military service seemed to do for his former pitchers. A second appearance was Cadore's last until the war ended. Ebbets scheduled "Cadore Day" and arranged a military ceremony and a doubleheader with the Pirates. Cadore gave up only two hits and a single run in eight innings. Lifted for a pinch hitter, "Caddy" did not get the decision. The Robins tied the game in the ninth and won it, 2-1, in twelve innings.

The Robins were to lose another pitcher to the war before the season ended. When Robinson heard that a pitcher named Harry Heitman, who was burning up the International League, lived in Brooklyn, the rookie was purchased for immediate delivery. Ebbets and Robinson were always looking for a local player, particularly a pitcher with an iron-man reputation. Heitman had already won seventeen games at Rochester and was leading the league in strikeouts. He reported to Ebbets Field on July 27 and was sent to the mound against the Cardinals. He got the leadoff man, but the next four batters hit safely and Robbie sent him to an early shower. Heitman dressed and the next day changed uniforms, donning a sailor's suit. He never returned to the major leagues. He remained a lifetime resident of Brooklyn, dying there in 1958. Neighbors, tactfully, never said much about the one-third of an inning he had pitched back in 1918, or his 108.00 ERA. Today he'd be paid to sign autographs at collectibles shows.

Burleigh Grimes made good with nineteen wins for a second-division team, just as Robinson had expected. However, the other starters all fell below the .500 mark. Larry Cheney was 11-13, Jack Coombs 8-14, and Rube Marquard lost eighteen while winning only nine, although four of these were shutouts.

One staff hopeful was Rusty Griner, bought from the minors after the Cardinals had given up on him. In 1913 he had lost a league-leading 22 games, and this was read by Ebbets and Robinson as a sign of a good pitcher with a bad team. Griner was also built to Robinson specifications. A righthander, he was 6-foot-1-1/2 and weighed over 200 pounds. On May 6, Griner had a no-hit game with two out in the ninth inning against the Phillies. Then Gavvy Cravath singled. Griner's victory was his only win of the season against five losses.

The 1918 season is a strange one in baseball's history. Because of America's involvement in the Great War, the game was considered by many to be a misuse of manpower. If a man could play big league baseball, why wasn't he in uniform fighting for his country? Secretary of War Newton Baker blew the whistle early. He proclaimed that after September 1, 1918, it was "work or fight." Able-bodied men were expected to do their part. The major leagues quickly fell into line. The season was cut to 126 games and ended on Labor Day. Jake Daubert viewed the decision to stop play early as a violation of the contract he had signed. He argued that the government didn't decree that big league baseball must stop by that date. Baker had only said players were subject to military duty if not employed in a war industry. It was Jake's argument that baseball could have played the regular 154-game schedule, using older players, such as himself, and young ones or minor leaguers. Daubert lost the argument.

Baker allowed players on the Red Sox and Cubs to delay complying with the work-or-fight order until the World Series was played. August was a hot month and Labor Day came with the nation in a hot spell. Play was desultory and the Red Sox beat the Cubs in six games. Babe Ruth and Carl Mays each won two games. Barely more than 15,000 fans turned out to see the Red Sox win the final game.

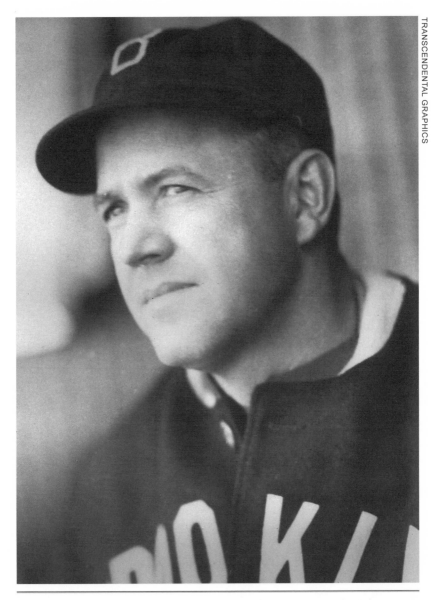

Big, tough, prickly spitballer Burleigh Grimes pitched nine seasons for Robinson in Brooklyn, and remains one of the Dodgers' all-time greatest hurlers. He returned as manager in the late '30s, when this photo was taken.

The Great War ended November 11, 1918, and the ballplayers came home. The season had been a bad one for the owners. Gate receipts were drastically off. The owners decided to tighten up in 1919, fearing that returning veterans, looking for jobs and ready to resume their war-interrupted lives, would stay away from the ballparks. The baseball moguls decided to play another short schedule of 140 games, ending on Labor Day. Rosters were cut from twenty-five players to twenty-one and salaries were reduced. Ebbets sent Daubert to Cincinnati for Tommy Griffith, who would be a solid outfield performer for many years. Griffith's grandson is Matt Williams, the Gold Glove third baseman and power hitter of the 1990s.

Daubert played first base for the Reds with his old smoothness and helped them to a surprise pennant of their own and a victory in the tainted 1919 World Series against the Chicago White Sox (later called the Black Sox when it was learned that a number of their players had negotiated, accepted, or known about gamblers' bribes to throw the Series).

In 1919 the Robins took longer to fall out of contention than they had the previous year. All the same, they ended up fifth again, racked with injuries. Robinson had to keep moving players to unfamiliar positions to keep nine able-bodied men on the field. At least retrospectively, one bright spot came during a Pittsburgh Pirate visit to Ebbets Field. On his third turn at bat in an otherwise forgettable game, former Robin Casey Stengel doffed his cap and released a somewhat battered sparrow he had concealed there. Casey had improvised the stunt when he saw a fallen bird fluttering in the outfield grass. He scooped it into his cap and took it to the dugout. He reckoned it had flown into a fence and would recover. The Casey-and-the-bird story became a staple of baseball storytelling and a classic Stengel tale. In telling the yarn in the years ahead, Casey would swear he'd put the bird under his hat for safekeeping and forgotten it was there. He was as surprised when it flew away as anyone, he would say, with a broad wink.

It is easy to smudge the 1918 and 1919 seasons together. Brooklyn finished fifth both years, but Robinson was not simply marking time. He was impatient with the injuries that hampered his team. He liked what he had. He was ready to spring another surprise on the competition. He just needed healthy players playing their proper positions.

14.

1920 – PIVOTAL CHANGES

Nineteen-twenty is probably baseball's most eventful season. It is the beginning of the long-ball era, with Babe Ruth's astonishing home run totals signaling the change in batting styles. From choke hitters punching singles over the infielders' heads, the game shifted to sluggers trying to duplicate the Babe's drives over the fences. The spitball was forbidden except for seventeen hurlers "grandfathered" because it was their bread-and-butter pitch. Nobody could legally scuff, shine, stain, or deface a ball either. The season would require an additional 10,000 baseballs as umpires began discarding any ball for any defect. It was the year of major league baseball's only death on the diamond and the year that the infamy of throwing the previous World Series was revealed. And, while hardly in a class with 1920's other significant events, Robinson sold his Baltimore-based butter and egg business. His decision signaled a personal optimism about the Dodgers .

Let Robbie make his case for the coming season as he did to Abe Yager in the March 29 edition of the Brooklyn *Eagle*. Brooklyn had just won five straight spring training games from the New York Yankees. They would travel north with the team that now showcased Babe Ruth at every stop, and would play a final three exhibition games at Ebbets Field. Sitting in the lobby of the Hotel Seminole, headquarters for the Brooklyn team, Robinson proposed, "Let's look at last year. We started the season crippled, became crippleder in mid-season and ended up the crippledest outfit in the land. Yet we finished fifth, only a few games behind Pittsburgh and Chicago.

"Look us over," he urged. "Not a cripple in the lot and all mentally and physically sound. Compare them to last spring. A busted infield and a catching staff not up to a hard race. Then Marquard broke his leg and Grimes went off his feed. Pfeffer got sick and a lot of other things happened. Later, when we had a look for third place, Grimes was spiked, the catching slowed up and the whole outfit went flooie.

"We led the league with base hits, and had an average of nine per game. We had the most putouts, with 3,829, although we had the most errors with 219. We played the longest game—that 20-inning battle with the Phillies. We rolled up the biggest score, 18-3 against the Braves. That's going some for a crippled team. And now, let's look them over individually.

"Ivan Olson made the greatest number hits of all sorts and the most singles. Hy Myers led the league in triples and runs batted in. He led in total bases, too. Rube Marquard had 10 strikeouts in a game before he got hurt. That's what a bunch of cripples did."

Robinson's optimism was shared by *The Sporting News*. Its editorial pointed out, "... they have a pitching staff that is the envy of all rivals, they have catching that should be much improved, their infield has been straightened out and the outfield is certainly no weaker than last year.

"Meanwhile," concluded TSN, "your Uncle Robbie has sold his poultry business and is devoting all his time to his ball club. Keep your eyes on him."

Robinson began 1920 by signing a one-year contract and announcing that he might leave baseball for a butter-and-egg business in Baltimore. He had mixed feelings about the future. He relished running the Dodgers, but the comforts of home in Baltimore and the opportunities to hunt and fish and play golf year-round tempted him. Ma went to Brooklyn with Robbie, but never let him forget that it required living in a rented house or, later, a hotel suite, almost half the year. When he pined for an

Leon Cadore achieved baseball immortality in 1920 by pitching the longest game in major league history–a twenty-six-inning 1-1 tie against Joe Oeschger of the Boston Braves.

alternate life style, it wasn't just to negotiate a better contract.

Spring training took place at Clearwater, Florida. Unlike the previous year, when Robinson came to camp almost blind in one eye from a hunting accident, this spring's scrutiny would be clear and approving. He was already headed south by train, having stopped off at Dover Hall, his favorite hunting lodge outside Brunswick, Georgia, where he was met by Rube Marquard. Rube's broken leg showed no sign of weakness as he trudged the surrounding countryside with Robbie.

Ebbets had insured harmony in camp by increasing everyone's salaries. There were fourteen holdovers from 1919, including the entire starting lineup, and twenty-eight new players for Robinson to look over. Outfielder Tommy Griffith was the only absentee. He was not arguing about salary. Like Robbie, he had an off-season career and was ready to make it a full-time occupation. His resolve was so strong that Robinson was thinking of trading one of his pitchers for a suitable replacement. The Dodgers opened the season with a rookie in Griffith's place. He was Bernie Neis, one project Robbie could never master. A combination of independent thinker and flake, he teetered on the brink of stardom for five years. He had great speed but Robinson's teams didn't steal bases. They would be last in 1920 with only seventy. Neis was a switch-hitter. Robbie wanted him to bat lefthanded only. Despite lining a home run over the short right field wall at Ebbets Field while batting lefthanded in an early game, the obdurate Neis insisted on taking cuts from the right side after that. Robinson yearned for Griffith, now a stockbroker in Cincinnati.

Spring training followed a formula dating back to Robinson's days with the Orioles. With one exception: the usual squad game on St. Patrick's Day between Irish players and others was called off. Unlike the old Orioles, the Robins could produce only four Irishmen.

In another break from tradition, the ballplayers played golf. Robinson's mastery of the Scots' game was evident. He won about every tournament for ballplayers, and he and catcher Ernie Krueger defeated the Yankees' Del Pratt and Bob Shawkey eleven up in a four-ball match at the Florida Country Club.

On links and diamond, Brooklyn's dominance of the Yankees continued as the teams traveled north. On March 20, while Brooklyn extended its winning streak, and Pfeffer, Smith, and Cadore held Ruth to a single and the Yankees to one run, a heckler lured the Babe into the stands. Ruth and coach Charley O'Leary were confronted by a knife-wielding antagonist. Ruth and O'Leary retreated. No arrest was made by the Clearwater police.

As March moved along Ruth was still without a home run, having been held to five singles in his first twenty-one times at bat against Brooklyn pitching. Then the Babe broke the ice. On April 2, he hit a home run over the center field fence 429 feet away. In the next games Ruth was still held to the occasional single until an overflow crowd in Winston-Salem, packing the ballpark to honor native son Ernie Shore, made it necessary to call any fly ball that reached the stands in right field a ground rule double. Ruth hit a pair. The first "double" went over the heads of everyone, and the baseball writers estimated it would have landed in the bleachers at the Polo Grounds where Ruth would play seventy-seven home games in 1920.

A chilled crowd of 10,000 was on hand as Brooklyn, having won the exhibition series with the Yankees, ten games to six, opened the season with the Phillies. Leon Cadore won the opener and Robinson then rotated his veterans, spotting them effectively, to build up an early season lead, winning eight of eleven games.

Then came "the odyssey to nowhere." On May 1, Brooklyn played the longest game ever, a twenty-six- inning 1-1 tie at Braves Field. Cadore probably shortened his career by going the full distance. He would be 15-14 in 1920, but it was his last winning season. Not so for his opponent, Joe Oeschger, previously a run-of-the-mill pitcher for the Phillies, who had just been acquired by the Braves. He had a winning season in 1920 and his only twenty-win season the next year. Cadore and Oeschger have been linked in trivia history ever since. They both went the twenty-six-inning distance before umpire Barry McCormick mercifully called a halt because of darkness. Even so, Ivy Olson, an Ernie Banks type who could never play enough games, begged for one more inning.

"Then we can say we played three games in one," he argued. He lost his plea and the Brooklyn players climbed aboard a night train to Brooklyn to play a single Sunday game before returning to resume the series with Boston. On the way to the railroad station, the Dodgers deposited Cadore at the team's Boston hotel. Caddy was put to bed, and told to rest and get plenty of sleep.

In the Sunday game with the Phillies, the Dodgers went thirteen more innings as Grimes lost, 4-3. Back in Boston they found Cadore still in bed. On Monday, Sherry Smith lost, 2-1, in nineteen innings. The Dodgers had played fifty-eight innings in three games and won none of them. (They also lost the makeup game for the tie on June 25.) It might have been enough to break the team's spirit, but Robbie saw that it didn't. He determined to patch the weakness in his lineup and made the return of Tommy Griffith his goal as the team set out on its first western swing.

Ebbets joined the team when it stopped in Cincinnati, Griffith's home city. The stockbroker was soon convinced his return would insure a pennant and bring him a World Series check. A week later he took his regular place in right field. With Myers in center and Wheat in left, the Dodgers' outfield was formidable once again.

It was the infield that improved the most under Robinson's artful juggling of players. Jimmy Johnston had shown over the years that he could play anywhere. By a season's end he could be considered a regular without having established himself at any one position. When Robbie stationed him at third base full-time, Johnston found his home. He was brilliant on defense and continued to be a strong batter.

At second base, Robinson played the agile Pete Kilduff, whom he had wangled out of Chicago in the final weeks of the previous season. While Kilduff didn't bring about a radical change in the erratic Ivy Olson at short, he seemed to steady him. After years of searching for a big league shortstop, Robbie settled for one who wasn't the worst in the league, although he was far from ranking with glovemen like Rabbit Maranville and Dave Bancroft. Ivy's reputation was damaged by the many routine ground balls he let roll between his legs. Robinson settled for Olson's bat in the lineup

Shortstop was almost always a problem for Robinson, and for many seasons
Ivy Olson was the adequate incumbent. A decent hitter, his defense was unreliable,
but his pugnacious attitude appealed to his manager.

and his driving personality on the field. Even if Ivy had to stuff cotton in his ears to muffle the taunts of the fans, he always played his hardest. Robbie never found his great shortstop, so often considered the key to a winning team. Ivy Olson filled the position well enough to hold on for many seasons.

A seasoned pro, Ed Konetchy, had been obtained in 1919 to replace the disgruntled Jake Daubert at first. Big Ed was a solid performer with good power. He didn't cover a lot of ground but he caught what he could reach.

The other weakness of the 1919 team had been behind the plate. Robinson had the veteran Otto Miller healthy and back again as the first-string catcher. His golfing partner, Ernie Krueger, returned to share catching roles. The third catcher, defensive specialist Rowdy Elliott, gave Robbie the edge he wanted. As a receiver himself, Robbie knew that some pitchers simply worked better with a preferred catcher. In 1920 he could again match starters against teams they were most likely to beat, and catchers with pitchers who worked best with them. Wilbert Robinson could not have spelled "symbiotic," but instinctively he knew what it meant. In 1920 it would mean a pennant. Six of his starters recorded wins in double figures.

15.

RUTH DWARFS BROOKLYN'S PENNANT

The Robins seemed to be marking time, waiting for Tommy Griffith to report. While he was back in Brooklyn working out at Ebbets Field, the winning pace of his teammates slowed against western division opponents. By the time Griffith considered himself ready to play, the club had slipped to fourth place. They were 16-13 going into the last weekend of May. Pittsburgh was in first place and Cincinnati and Chicago were also ahead of Brooklyn. On Sunday, May 30, the Robins won and edged up to third. On May 31, they won the Decoration Day doubleheader from the New York Giants behind Grimes and Cadore, and tied for first.

June began with Brooklyn taking sole possession of first place, rallying with three ninth-inning runs in an Ebbets Field comeback win, 10-9. More important, perhaps, was that Tommy Griffith made his first appearance of 1920 with a leadoff pinch-hit single to start the rally. Now Robinson could play his best lineup. It must have cheered him, forced as he was to manage in street clothes because of gout, to put Jimmy Johnston at third base again, move Pete Kilduff from third back to second, and fan out his regular outfield of Wheat, Myers, and Griffith.

The Robins clung to a slim lead as the tight pennant race continued through June. Brooklyn bats went cold and the team lost nine of twelve games at home. They dropped to third, then, after losing five of six games in Boston, down to fourth, only a half-game out of sixth place. As July began, the pitching took hold again. Marquard avenged a June 13 loss on Marquard Day at Ebbets Field. (He had been given a diamond stickpin but no runs as he lost, 1-0.) On July 1 the Rube's four-hitter at the Polo Grounds was Brooklyn's third win in a row.

Clouds of suspicion began to form in baseball's firmament. Benny Kauff, the one-time Federal League star rumored to be an untrustworthy fellow, was waived out of the majors despite hitting two home runs in his final big league game.

The Robins won a July 4 doubleheader to move into second place behind the defending champion Reds. The race seemed to be settling down to a fight between Brooklyn and Cincinnati, but the Giants began to gain ground on the leaders. The Robins headed off to face the dangerous western division clubs on July 6, a half-game behind. On July 10, they regained first place, splitting a doubleheader with St. Louis on Al Mamaux's nightcap shutout, while the Reds lost a single game.

Baseball fans were reacting to the astonishing talent of Babe Ruth. As the Robins got back into the lead, the headlines hailed Ruth's twenty-fifth home run, with half a season to play. His homer was cheered by members of the Knights of Columbus as they packed the Polo Grounds to cheer their fellow Knight. It is said that the Babe saved baseball after the scandal of the thrown 1919 World Series. Actually, he had already injected such excitement into the baseball scene that not even such a major disgrace could change it. In early 1920, before the Black Sox scandal had been bared, the public was avidly following the charismatic Ruth's slugging. Even when Brooklyn had played its twenty-six-inning game on May 1, the New York papers headlined Ruth's first home run as a Yankee. After that, as the Babe lofted home run after home run over fences and into bleacher seats, the fans' first question when the scores came in was, "Did Ruth hit one today?"

While the ball club was away, Ebbets Field was used for other purposes. It was an Olympic year, and a track meet was staged in the ballpark. Charlie Paddock, soon to be called "the world's fastest human" after winning the 100-meter dash later that year at the Antwerp Olympics, won his specialty over rival Jackson Scholz. The next day it was baseball again as the Bacharach Giants broke even in a doubleheader in what was considered "The Colored World Series."

By mid-July, Brooklyn seemed to have hit a pennant-winning stride. They had won seventeen of their last twenty, taking five out of six from Chicago, losing only to Grover Cleveland Alexander. A tough set of games with the Reds, with Grimes winning the opener and Cadore topping Jimmy Ring the next day, failed to kill off Cincinnati. Dolf Luque topped Sherry Smith and the Robins with four—rather than the usual two—umpires working the game. The quartet of men in blue—Cy Rigler, Charlie Moran, Pete Harrison, and Bob Hart—were stationed with two in the infield and two on the foul lines where standing-room fans might interfere with balls in play. The series ended with Grimes winning the final game from Hod Eller. Brooklyn held a seemingly safe four-game lead. Ebbets advised fans to hold their ticket stubs to identify themselves as regular team supporters. He didn't want the scalpers to grab blocks of seats through political contacts as they had in 1916.

Joy in Flatbush was muted when word came on August 17 that Ray Chapman had been killed by a lethal pitch thrown by Carl Mays, now playing for the Yankees. Assuming the loss of Chapman would end Cleveland's hopes for a pennant, the Robins began to figure the White Sox as their Series opponents. But Cleveland located a future Hall of Fame shortstop, Joe Sewell, just out of the University of Alabama, and continued to battle Chicago to the wire.

The mid-August euphoria faded quickly. The Reds refused to fold and the Giants were closing the gap. McGraw's team had been flat the first half of the season, particularly missing Frank Frisch, whose broken leg didn't heal until only eight weeks were left in the season.

Brooklyn's four-game lead melted when the team lost four of six in Pittsburgh. The western trip over, Brooklyn, after an opening Grimes shutout, lost three in a row to the Reds. The lead was only half a game—and the Giants continued to gain.

But Robinson steadied his troops and they fought back. The Reds faded from contention and the Giants could not gain as the

Robins matched late victories with them. Rube Marquard delivered the season's coup de grâce to McGraw's hopes on September 26 when he shut out New York. After this game, an ecstatic Robinson gleefully exited Ebbets Field, looking for Ma. She was standing next to a strange woman, whom the distracted Uncle Robbie mistakenly hugged and kissed, thinking she was his wife.

The next day, while Brooklyn was idle, New York lost in Boston and the "next year" for which Brooklyn had waited had arrived. The team that had waived Marquard goodbye in 1915 fell to seven behind in the final standings. Cincinnati was a further three and a half back in third place.

The 1920 race appears an almost easy win for the Robins. They never had a long losing streak and one of their strong starters was always certain to stop any skid. The press gave the credit to Robinson for his artful guidance of a team that was soundly assembled and led.

The team gathered before the next day's game, but there were none of the celebrations that might have been expected. Just as John McGraw had "piddled" on his 1916 pennant, an even greater distraction claimed the nation's attention. The day Brooklyn won the pennant, the headline of the Philadelphia *North American* claimed: Gamblers Promised White Sox $100,000 to Lose.

As Robinson gathered his players around him, they were all wondering if the World Series would be canceled. The White Sox, even if stripped of half their stars, might yet win the American League pennant. How could they be allowed to participate under the circumstances?

While the nation wondered who would face the Robins in the World Series, if one were held, the final American League games were played. The unthinkable did not happen. The Cleveland Indians, led by manager Tris Speaker, won their first pennant.

Although we do not know his feelings about the "Black Sox," the Robins had among them a witness to the performance of the 1919 Chicago White Sox. Eddie Bennett, a dwarfed hunchback, was Brooklyn's mascot and insurer of good luck. He had been similarly connected, even if only for a few games, with the 1919 White Sox.

A fifteen-year-old orphan who was virtually a street waif, he had hung around New York area ballparks. One day his life's work began. Happy Felsch, star center fielder of the Chicago White Sox, spotted the boy in the bleachers at Yankee Stadium. Noticing the hump on the youngster's back, Happy Felsch shouted up to him, "Hey boy. Are you lucky?" Bennett assured the White Sox outfielder that he was. Felsch brought the youngster from the bleachers to the White Sox bench, where he was welcomed by all hands. Most of them briskly rubbed the hump on his back for good luck. In those times, sensitivity to the feelings of the handicapped and minorities was not a general concern. Chicago had lost the first game of a doubleheader that day, but with Eddie Bennett casting his spells and putting hex signs on the Yankee pitchers, they drubbed New York in the second contest. The youngster was asked to come back the next day and repeat his good luck routines. Again, the White Sox had a field day against the Yankees. When Chicago left that night for Philadelphia, they took Eddie Bennett with them.

It is only two hours by train from Philadelphia back to New York City, and it is unlikely that Bennett went any farther with the White Sox. He is not in the 1919 White Sox team picture, which usually showed batboys and mascots. None of the World Series action photos or 1919 photos of the White Sox at the National Baseball Library and Archive shows Eddie Bennett. Nonetheless, according to a 1924 writeup in the New York *Sun*, he served as mascot for five straight pennant-winners: the White Sox in 1919 (for at least a little while), the Dodgers in 1920, and the Yankees in 1921, '22, and '23. It is supposed to have been Hy Myers who spotted the "lucky" hunchback and took him into Ebbets Field.

Meanwhile, a backlash of suspicion that all ball clubs had been corrupted by gamblers cast a shadow over the Dodgers. When the New York *Evening Sun* passed along rumors that the same clique of gamblers was trying to get the Brooklyn players to throw the 1920 World Series, David Lewis, the Brooklyn district attorney, made political capital in the press. He announced he would bring Ebbets, Robinson, and the players to his office and grill them about their possible involvement with gamblers.

Ebbets bristled. "The boys of the Brooklyn baseball team are as clean-cut and as honest fellows as can be found anywhere in the world of athletics," he announced. After the questioning, Lewis agreed they were as honest as Ebbets said they were. Robbie looked on the inquiry as another way to piddle on his pennant.

16.

THE CURSE OF THE MASCOT

Brooklyn was slightly favored by the baseball press to win the 1920 World Series, which, like those of 1919 and 1921, was a best-five-of-nine affair. But the fans' sympathy was with the Cleveland Indians. Since Ray Chapman's fatal beaning by Carl Mays, fans everywhere had rooted for the Indians. The success of his rookie replacement, Joe Sewell, raised their expectations. Playing manager Tris Speaker was still a superstar. The lineup that would face Brooklyn was potent. "The Gray Eagle" arranged his outfield according to who pitched for the other team. Charley Jamieson and Steve Evans platooned in left, and Elmer Smith, Jack Graney, and the former pitching ace of the Red Sox, Joe Wood, all saw service in right. Smokey Joe's arm had been so badly injurerd that he could barely throw the ball back to the infield, but his bat was potent.

Jimmy Johnston's brother, Doc Johnston, shared Indians first base duties with George "Tioga" Burns. The Johnston brothers were the first siblings to face each other in the championship Series. Second baseman Bill Wambsganss, a player whose name would be immortalized in trivia questions, was a fine fielder and fair batsman. He appeared in box scores as "Wamby." Joe Sewell was now playing an inspired game at shortstop. At third base was a Brooklyn nemesis, Larry Gardner. In the 1916 World Series, playing for the Red Sox, Gardner had hit two home runs and led all players with six runs batted in. Steve O'Neill and Les Nunamaker shared the catching. The fans and players had not forgotten Ray Chapman, of course, and the Indians wore a black mourning band on their left sleeves.

Cleveland had fewer strong pitchers than Brooklyn, but its three double-figure winners all had twenty or more victories. Jim Bagby led with thirty-one wins, spitballer Stan Coveleski had won twenty-four, and Ray Caldwell twenty. There had been no fourth starter on the staff until the late-season addition of Duster Mails in August. Robinson remembered Mails, who had dubbed himself "the Great" when he joined Brooklyn in 1915. He would call himself "the Great Mails" during a long career in the Pacific Coast League. It was his high inside pitch that caused batters to call him "Duster."

The Robins opened the Series at home, introducing new cream-colored uniforms with dark pinstripes. Pinstripes are supposed to make the wearer appear slimmer, but this sartorial tip never applied to the rotund Robbie. Tuesday, October 5, was a raw day. New York Mayor John Hylan entered Ebbets Field waving a Brooklyn pennant. The trumpets of the police department band blew a fanfare as the mayor bowed to the chilled crowd. Hylan, in public view, had to keep warm as best he could. Up in the press box each writer was slipped a half-pint of whiskey with Ebbets' compliments. They sipped gratefully throughout the game. One writer was so appreciative that he stated his approval of Charlie's kindness in his story of the game. Unfortunately, Prohibition had become the law of the land, and the next day the federal government raided Ebbets Field. Treasury agents, blue noses sniffing suspiciously, searched the press area and even ransacked Ebbets' private office. Charlie, of course, had been tipped off to the raid and had moved the booze to safety.

Although Burleigh Grimes had won twenty-one games and led the league with a .676 winning percentage, Robinson gave the opening assignment to the more experienced Rube Marquard. Speaker responded by withholding his ace Bagby and starting Coveleski. Both Stan and Burleigh relied on the spitball as their money pitch, and both were among the hurlers allowed to continue throwing the outlawed pitch.

Ivy Olson lost little time in giving Cleveland a break it capitalized on. When George Burns' windblown pop fly fell beyond the reach of the lumbering Ed Konetchy, Ivy watched in bemusement. The first baseman rifled a throw to second base to stop Burns from advancing. Alas, Ivy Olson had not covered the bag. Burns scored as the throw ended up in the left field corner. As he often did, Olson immediately turned in a dazzling play to get the first out of the inning. However, Joe Wood walked and young Joe Sewell rifled a single to move him to third. Steve O'Neill doubled to left and Wood scored with Sewell stopping at third. Coveleski grounded to first baseman Konetchy who stepped on the base and threw to the plate. Sewell stopped and tried to get back to third base but was tagged out in a rundown. Cleveland led, 2-0.

Coveleski had the Dodgers swinging feebly at his diving spitters. Cleveland added a third run in the fourth inning on doubles by Wood and O'Neill. Wheat scored Brooklyn's only run in the seventh. After doubling to lead off, he moved to third on an infield out and scored on another.

Down a game in a best-of-nine series wasn't too severe a handicap, the Dodger fans assured themselves. "Boily'll get 'em tomorrow," they promised each other in the patois of Flatbush. Robbie sent his ace Burleigh Grimes to the mound in Game 2. Jim Bagby held Brooklyn to three scattered runs, but Grimes was more effective in the clutch and shut out the Indians on seven hits.

Sherry Smith, whom Robinson favored in must-win situations, again rose to the occasion and won a tough third game, 2-1. Brooklyn's pair of runs came in the first inning off Ray Caldwell. Duster Mails came in to relieve and stopped the Robins cold. He turned them back inning after inning while Smith did the same to Cleveland. The Indians threatened in the fifth when Sewell walked and O'Neill singled with one out. Mails, insisting he was as good a hitter as a pitcher, hit the ball sharply only to have Ivy Olson turn it into a spectacular double play. Cleveland threatened again in the eighth. With one out, O'Neill got his second single. Les

Nunamaker, batting for Mails, hit into another double play, ending the inning. Dodger fans held their breath as Smith set down the Indians in the ninth to complete a masterful performance, getting twenty ground-ball outs. The Dodgers led the Series, two games to one.

Now came what only a few understand to be the turning point of the World Series. Since the owners had decided that a best-of-nine Series would bring in more money than the standard best-of-seven games, there would now be four straight games in Cleveland. "Wait for us here," mascot Eddie Bennett was told. "We'll be back to wrap up the Series, if we don't win it in Cleveland." Bennett's face grew dark. He had expected, as a reward for the good luck hump rubbings he had endured, that he would travel to Cleveland with the team. He felt betrayed, and he was angry.

"A coise on youse," Bennett swore in Brooklynese. He left the bats and equipment for someone else to pack and ship to Cleveland. He was finished with the ungrateful Dodgers. As Red Sox fans have chalked up their team's troubles to the "Curse of the Bambino," and Cleveland rooters talked for years about the "Curse of Rocky Colavito," why can't Brooklynites, with much more direct evidence, claim the "Curse of the Mascot?"

We don't know how young Eddie spent his time after the World Series. With the Dodgers under his spell, he probably chanted incantations, perhaps danced around a cauldron of vitriol. How he survived the winter, we can only guess. However, the baseball world knows that the next season he persuaded the New York Yankees that, indeed, he had the power to bring good luck or, if he was crossed, bad. He had only to point out that, once he had jinxed his former employers, they went to Cleveland without him and lost four straight games and the World Series.

With the Yankees, Eddie Bennett became the best-known mascot of all time. They didn't object to paying his travel expenses to the next three World Series. Their opponents were the New York Giants and subway fare to the Polo Grounds was only a nickel.

No one ever accepted the blame for the costly blunder of snubbing the team's good luck charm. The public couldn't believe it of

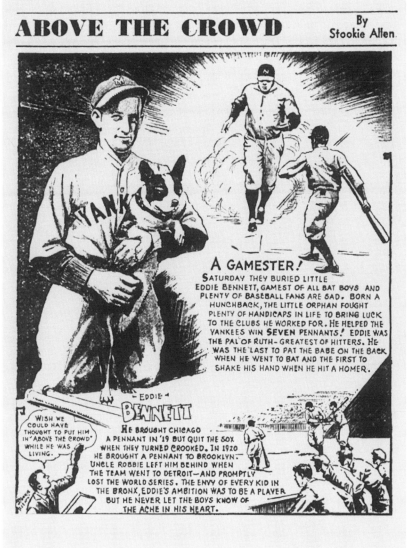

A sentimental and error-ridden obituary cartoon for the man who "cursed" the Dodgers.

the beloved Uncle Robbie. They assumed he just hadn't thought about the mascot, being too busy working on his pitching rotation for the rest of the Series. They could believe it of Ebbets. One of the pleasures of going to the ballpark was to heckle Ebbets about his tight-fistedness. He would shout back at his tormentors, "How come I'm the only big league owner without a car? I have to ride the trolley to the games."

The "Curse of the Mascot" took effect even before the first game was played in Cleveland. The first headline of the afternoon papers announced: Marquard Arrested As Ticket Scalper. Police claimed they heard Rube try to sell eight box seats for $350. They had been bought for $52.80. Rube, protesting that a mistake had been made, was released pending a hearing. The Rube, who despite his nickname was far from a bucolic hayseed, having become a New Yorker with a Broadway taste, went to the ballpark and even pitched three scoreless relief innings in a losing cause as Stan Coveleski again beat Brooklyn, 5-1. The Series was even and Eddie Bennett's hex was working.

Game 5 was one of the most memorable in the history of the World Series, but the Dodgers would have liked to forget it. Grimes started, but may not have had enough rest. The first two Indians batters singled and, on a sacrifice bunt by Tris Speaker, Grimes fell down in pursuit of the ball and the bases were full. Elmer Smith then stepped to the plate and hit the first grand slam home run in World Series history. It wasn't the only historic homer of the day for the Indians. In the fourth inning pitcher Jim Bagby drove a ball into an opening in the temporary stands in center field for the first World Series round-tripper by a pitcher.

The fates weren't through. Now trailing, 7-0, the Dodgers showed signs of life in the fifth. They opened with a pair of singles. Clarence Mitchell, who had relieved Grimes in the fourth, came to bat. He was a fine hitter, who sometimes even played first base and pinch hit for others. Robinson, sensing that he might be able to get the Dodgers going, called for the hit-and-run. The base runners, Kilduff and Miller, broke with the pitch and Mitchell swung. He hit a scorching line drive over second base. Wambsganss, dashing over to cover second on the play, leaped and made a one-hand catch. He came down almost on second base, kicked the sack to force Kilduff for out number two, and turned to find Otto Miller standing dumfounded a few feet away. Wamby reached out and touched the Dodger baserunner to complete what remains today the only unassisted triple play ever seen in a World Series.

In a 1935 column, sportswriter Frank Menke recalled an event that followed the game. Robinson, simmering over the way his team had lost such a critical game, returned to his hotel. A sympathetic bell captain provided the bourbon and ice, and Robbie sprawled in a chair to console himself. The more he drank the madder he got. When Menke arrived at the Robinson suite, intending to get the manager's views for the bylined column he was ghosting, he had to bang on the door to get a response.

"What the hell do you want?" Robinson demanded, blocking the doorway. Menke's reason did not impress the Dodger boss. He glared, swished the icy contents of his glass, and flung the bourbon highball at the reporter, who ducked as the drink went over his head. At that moment two strangers were passing in the hallway. One of them caught the full effect as Robbie's drink splashed down his suit.

"Who done that?" the outraged hotel guest demanded. Robinson had gone back inside and only Menke was standing outside the door. He thought quickly. "The guy who threw the drink is inside, but you don't want to disturb him. He's been drinking and gotten nasty. He happens to be Jack Dempsey," Menke improvised. At the thought of the heavyweight champ charging at them, the men hurried down the stairs. They didn't wait for the elevator, but descended six steps at a time.

The next day the Dodgers ran into Duster Mails again. Although Sherry Smith limited the Indians to only two runs, Mails pitched a three-hit shutout. In a best-of-seven Series, it would have been all over. But Cleveland still needed another victory.

Even before the Dodgers went to the ballpark the next afternoon, Marquard had his day in court. A Cleveland municipal judge listened while the pitcher explained he was just trying to dispose of one ticket, at face value, for a friend. Cleveland had the home-court advantage and the Rube was found guilty of scalping and fined $25. A few hours later, his teammates plodded through nine more scoreless innings. Stan Coveleski won his third game and closed out the Series.The Indians had swept four straight from Brooklyn.

Ebbets had always been careful to leave team discipline to his manager. The Marquard scalping incident, however, outraged him. He had warned his Brooklyn patrons to identify themselves and get World Series tickets at regular box-office prices. He hadn't anticipated chicanery in Cleveland, certainly not by one of his own players. A self-made man who lived on the earnings of his ball club, he savored the company of the wealthy men who owned the other teams. Marquard had embarrassed Ebbets where it hurt the most.

Just before Christmas, Ebbets gave himself a present. He'd once swapped Casey Stengel to the Cincinnati Reds to rid himself of a player who embarrassed him. Now he disposed of Marquard the same way. As he had in getting Tommy Griffith for Casey, he got value for Marquard from Cincinnati. Dutch Ruether had led the Reds to the pennant in 1919 with 19 wins and six losses. In 1920 he was 16-12. Perhaps the Reds thought he was slipping. He would be a twenty-one-game winner for Robinson in 1922 and, after being traded, helped pitch the Washington Senators to the 1925 pennant with an 18-7 record. He finished his career going 13-6 with the great 1927 New York Yankees.

"The Curse of the Mascot" had long-lasting results. The 1920 flag was the last pennant won by a Brooklyn team until 1941 and a World Championship flag would not fly over Ebbets Field until 1955. The expletives that followed Walter O'Malley as he took the Dodgers away from their faithful Brooklyn followers were the culminating curse.

17.

DAZZY ARRIVES

Spring training, 1921, was marred by the absence of Burleigh Grimes. He rejected Ebbets' contract offer and prepared to spend the season on his farm. A cold silence settled over the impasse until a worried Robinson urged Ebbets to give in. Grimes signed the night before the season opened and came ready to pitch the first game. He led the way early in the season as the champion Robins appeared headed for a repeat title. In late April and into May they won eleven straight and, after a loss to the Giants, won four more in a row. They were a close second when they fell apart.

There were no obvious reasons for the whole team going flat. No injuries, no fights, no factions. The whole team just played poorly. Looking for solutions, Robinson juggled the roster. He sold Ed Konetchy to the Phillies and gave utility man Ray Schmandt the first base job. As a regular, he batted .306. Jeff Pfeffer, 1-5, was traded to the Cardinals, where he went 9-3 the rest of the way and won nineteen the next year. Brooklyn got a well-traveled utility infielder, Hal Janvrin, and a wild and erratic lefthander, Ferdie Schupp, who'd had one brilliant season with the Giants before wildness undid him. Robinson failed to help Schupp locate home plate. The second guessers agreed he had made a bad deal.

The early 1920s belonged to the Giants in the National League. They won four consecutive pennants. The Dodgers were not as bad as their three second-division finishes suggest. They lost only two more games than they won in 1921, '22, and '23, despite a fifth-place and two sixth-place finishes. (Relations between McGraw and Robinson during these years remained chilly. In the winter of 1922, McGraw hosted a reunion of the famous old Orioles. For convenience, they gathered at the Robinson house on St. Paul Street in Baltimore. Robinson and McGraw were civil. They climbed into a tally-ho with their old manager, Ned Hanlon, Robbie's battery mate Sadie McMahon, Dirty Jack Doyle, and Steve Brodie. Dan Brouthers, whom McGraw had given a gate-keeper's job at the Polo Grounds, was too ill to attend. Wee Willie Keeler, too, was sick and died soon after the reunion.)

Robinson tinkered with his 1922 lineup, but he lacked key elements until a chain of events led him to one of the great finds of all time. Otto Miller's legs were getting weary and he had man-agerial ambitions. He didn't want or expect to dislodge Robbie, but he hoped for a minor league managerial spot as soon as Ebbets could get a replacement for him. A highly regarded catching prospect, Hank DeBerry, was with New Orleans in the Southern Association. His contract was for sale, but only as part of a pack-age deal. For $10,000, Ebbets could buy both DeBerry and pitcher Dazzy Vance. Vance, thirty-one, had bounced around the minors for years, failing in short stints with the Pirates and Yankees in 1915 and again with the Yankees in 1918.

Dazzy had strained his arm in 1914 by pitching four games in six days. After that, his arm usually gave out soon after a season began and he moved on to another team. He had drifted to New Orleans by 1920 and one night, playing poker with teammates, he banged his arm on the edge of the table while raking in a pot. When it still hurt in the morning, Vance went to a doctor, who diagnosed and treated an underlying problem that had been con-cealed until the bump. Dazzy was able to pitch again without pain. Of course, his reputation for previous failures was held against him, and Ebbets balked at the deal. He had been sold too many sore-armed pitchers.

It was DeBerry who insisted that anyone who wanted him had to take his mate. Robinson, of course, liked the deal. He had always believed in matching pitchers and catchers. Finally, Ebbets grudgingly gave in and bought the greatest pitcher Brooklyn ever had.

Beginning in 1922, Vance led the National League in strikeouts for seven years. He became almost as synonymous with speed as Walter Johnson, but he also threw a low-breaking curveball and a knuckleball for a changeup. Dazzy was wily, too. To take advantage of the shirt-sleeved fans sitting behind him in the bleachers, he sliced the sleeve of his sweat shirt into ribbons. The fatal beaning of Ray Chapman was fresh in everyone's mind, and Vance counted on that for intimidation. Eventually, the league ruled against the trick, realizing that the difficulty of picking up the ball coming out of a flapping background was an added danger.

Not that Dazzy Vance was vicious. He was anything but. A towering figure, he had curly reddish blonde hair and a florid complexion. Off the field he was a leader among the Robins' fun seekers. As a baseball veteran who offered to bet $100 he could join any team in any league and know at least three players as former teammates or opponents, he came to training camp already on a first-name basis with most of his teammates and was spared the usual rookie hazing.

During the 1920s, Vance's starring era, Brooklyn developed a deserved reputation as "the Daffy Dodgers." Clarence Arthur Vance usually was involved in team pranks. Although he was born in Hastings, Nebraska, Daz was a Florida "good ol' boy" by choice. He lived a rustic life in Homosassa Springs, north of Tampa. He met Robbie's social standards. His winters were spent hunting and fishing, and he had a taste for moonshine whiskey. That he was 6-foot-2 and weighed 200 pounds satisfied the Robinson expectations of a pitcher's physical appearance. Dazzy's pitching style was simple. He reared back, kicked his left foot high and catapulted the ball overhand. It exploded past the batter or swerved away. Although his speed excited the fans, it was his control of the curve that delighted his manager.

Another newcomer in 1922 was Handy Andy High, a 5-foot-5 lefthanded-hitting infielder. He eventually settled at third base, but he was part of Robinson's search for a shortstop more sure-handed than Ivy Olson. In 1922, Olson appeared in only fifty-one games at shortstop, moving to second for eighty-five. Jimmy Johnston played three infield positions, with High most often at third base. In 1923, Olson was virtually a bench warmer, as Robinson again tried to find a true major league shortstop.

Shufflin' Phil Douglas, who was now John McGraw's headache, spoiled Vance's 1922 debut with a 4-3 win. (Vance had started only once before in the major leagues, in 1915 with the Pittsburgh Pirates. Douglas had beaten him that day, too.) In August, however, while befuddled by drink and incensed at his treatment by McGraw, Phil, the Giants' leading pitcher at 11-3, decided he could hurt the Giants most by quitting the team. He wrote to his former Cub roommate, Les Mann, now with the Cardinals, and offered to "disappear" if Mann and his teammates would make it "worth his while." Mann showed the letter to Branch Rickey, his manager and a man of unrelenting principle. Rather than accept that poor Phil Douglas was an alcoholic who probably wasn't responsible for his actions and who certainly needed help, Rickey's conscience compelled him to turn the matter over to the new commissioner, Judge Kenesaw Mountain Landis. Equally moralistic, Landis banned Phil Douglas. He shuffled off into the darkness of semipro baseball.

While Vance brought some harmony to the Robins, not all his teammates were happy. Ol' Stubblebeard, Burleigh Grimes, was too fierce a competitor to laugh off lax play behind him. In August, Grimes was in an ugly mood when the Cincinnati Reds hit him hard in a game at Ebbets Field. Convinced some of the ground balls should have been fielded and turned into inning-ending double plays, "Boily berled over." Disgusted, he laid a fat pitch over the heart of the plate for the former Dodger captain, Jake Daubert. The ball cleared the right field fence to climax a six-run inning. When the carnage ended, Grimes stomped into the dugout. Robinson was waiting for him. The two stood jaw to jaw exchanging invective. The manager had learned his cuss words with the old Baltimore Orioles. Grimes invented his own.

Ebbets socked Burleigh with a $200 fine and issued a public reprimand. He instructed his pitcher to apologize to the manager and promise to avoid future swearing. To add salt to the fiscal wound, he concluded, "Pitch as manager Robinson advises." Grimes ended with seventeen victories to go with eighteen by Vance. Dutch Ruether topped the staff with twenty-one wins. Despite three strong starters, the team finished two games below .500, in sixth place.

The next Dodger with star quality was Jacques Fournier, acquired in a winter trade before the 1923 season. Called "Jack," he had been around the majors almost as long as Dazzy had been in the minors, and had recently become a long-ball threat. Robinson broke up his long established outfield of Wheat, Myers, and Griffith by trading Hy Myers to St. Louis for Fournier, sending Ray Schmandt along in the trade. Robbie had diagnosed Fournier's swing as ideally suited to the right field wall at Ebbets Field and was proved right. In his three seasons with the Robins, Fournier averaged twenty-four home runs. Few batters other than Ruth hit substantially more at the time. Fournier led the National League one year, was second another, and third in his final season in Brooklyn. Fournier was also a positive force on the team. He was liked by everyone. Only one situation wiped the smile off Fournier's face during the 1923 season. In a wild June game against the Phillies, Fournier made six hits in six times at bat and was at the plate again in the ninth inning. He was on the threshold of equaling Robinson's proudest record as a player. A slow runner was on first and Robinson sent him on a puzzling steal attempt that failed, ending the inning. Fournier wasn't puzzled. He blamed the manager for a bad call simply to keep his own seven-for-seven record from being tied.

A winter acquisition who lacked star quality but made up for it later by being the only major leaguer ever convicted of murder was Sam Crane. A shortstop whose promise had eluded development by Connie Mack and who had also failed in trials elsewhere, he appeared in three games in 1923. In 1930, Crane found his girlfriend in a hotel bed with another man and shot them both. He won parole in 1940 with Connie Mack as a character witness. Mack also gave him a job.

Zack Wheat showed no signs of slowing down. After he had led

TRANSCENDENTAL GRAPHICS

Well-liked, gentlemanly first baseman Jack Fournier developed into a slugger with Brooklyn. He led the National League in home runs with twenty-seven in 1924 and knocked in 130 runs in 1925.

the league in fielding average in 1922, while batting .335, Zack figured he was worth a $1,200 raise to $10,000. He sent Ebbets' first contract back and asked for more. Ebbets refused to yield. Spring training opened in Clearwater, where Ebbets had invested in the Florida land boom, figuring the presence of the Robins in training would attract others to build expensive homes there, too. A difference of $500 kept Wheat back on the farm. In a team meeting, the other players made Ebbets an offer they thought he couldn't refuse. They would chip in and make up the $500 difference. Ebbets finally gave in. He tacked on the $500 Wheat wanted. Zack rewarded the owner with his highest career average—.375.

The age of the Daffy Dodgers might have begun in the spring of 1923, when the Robins arrived to play an exhibition game with the Cleveland Indians. They were greeted by a surprised Tris Speaker.

"What are you doing here, Robbie?" he asked.

"Come to play you a ball game," answered Uncle Robbie.

"The game's tomorrow," laughed the Indians manager.

Robinson harrumphed his way back to the team bus followed by his snickering players.

The 1923 season had high spots, but not enough of them to avoid another sixth-place finish, again two games below the break-even mark. Opening day set a tone of unrealized promise for the season. Dutch Ruether, who had beaten the Phillies seven straight the year before, had to settle for a fourteen-inning tie.

In June, Sammy Bohne of the Reds spoiled a Vance bid for a no-hitter with a two-out single in the ninth. Vance was frustrated again when his ten-game winning streak was stopped by the Cardinals in August.

In midseason a college shortstop with a degree from Princeton became an unlikely addition to the Robins. The erudite Moe Berg remained an improbable major leaguer for the next sixteen seasons. Too slow to cover ground in the infield, he moved behind the plate, but his hitting never improved much. He hit .186 with the Dodgers. Brooklyn writers explained his failure to succeed by saying, "Moe Berg could speak a dozen languages, but he couldn't hit in any of them."

18.

ALMOST

Maybe Dazzy Vance took it as a wake-up call when, just before heading for spring training in 1924, he learned that the National League had voted to pay a $1,000 prize to the most valuable player of the coming season. Despite leading the league in strikeouts his first two years with the Robins, he had fallen short of the magic twenty-game level. For two sixth-place clubs, he'd managed eighteen victories. During spring training this year, though, Vance bet slugger Jack Fournier, who had hit twenty-two home runs in 1923, that he would win more games in 1924 than Fournier would hit homers.

The Robins showed little promise during training in Clearwater. Robinson did not like to work his veteran pitchers too much before the regular season began. The practice games were lost by aspiring rookie pitchers, while perspiring veterans ran laps around the outfield. When the Robins broke camp and played a losing string of games coming north, Brooklyn fans prepared for another lackluster campaign.

Ebbets began the season with another dispute with God's spokespersons. Protestant clergy were outraged when the season opened on Easter Sunday. Ebbets was glad to concede them the sunrise services. All he asked for was the afternoon in which to play a ball game. He was even pleased to eliminate the customary opening day ceremonies—saving himself the cost of a marching band—and the speeches and throwing out of the first ball by the borough president. There was simply the cry, "Play Ball," by the ump, and the hectic 1924 pennant race was on. The only ceremony was an imaginary one. A reporter "leaked" plans for the intended presentation of a new, extra-large belt to the Dodger manager before the flag raising.

"The new belt will be adjusted immediately after the flag-raising. The Brooklyn players and the visiting team in column of platoons will march twice around Uncle Wilbert while the band plays, 'It's A Long, Long Way To Tipperary'. After this the teams will separate, each holding an end of the belt and start tugging after the fashion of the tug-of-war teams. When the ends are brought together the buckle will be snapped into place and Uncle Wilbert will stand cinched for the rest of the season."

The new faces on the 1924 Robins were old faces in baseball. Rookies fell by the wayside. Shortstop was still a problem. Ivy Olson finally disappeared after only ten games, and Robinson installed Johnny Mitchell, who couldn't win a starting job with the Yankees or Red Sox. He couldn't win one with Brooklyn, either. Shortstop was passed around from Mitchell to Andy High to Jimmy Johnston and whoever else was available. Fournier played first base, Milt Stock, in the league since 1912, played third base satisfactorily, and Andy High divided his games between short and second base.

The outfield was much more settled, with captain Wheat in left and Tommy Griffith in right flanking the speedy Bernie Neis or Eddie Brown. Ebbets had bought Brown from Indianapolis where the Giants had sent him to improve the throwing ability that had earned him the nickname, "Glass Arm Eddie." Zack Taylor did most of the catching, with Hank DeBerry handling Vance and occasionally others.

Vance and Grimes would have their best seasons in 1924 en route to baseball's Hall of Fame, but the staff lacked depth. The team didn't jell until Robinson got Bill Doak in mid-June. Spittin' Bill Doak, another of the grandfathered spitballers, had long been one of the best pitchers in the league. He had been the star of the St. Louis Cardinals staff, twice winning twenty games and twice leading the league in ERA. In recent seasons he had slipped below .500 and was considered washed up. The Cards were willing to pass him along to the Robins in exchange for a pitcher of limited promise and grammar—Len Dickerman, who had foretold his own demise by observing, "On this club, it's every man for their selves."

Once Doak arrived, the Dodgers began to move up. In late June, as the Giants won their tenth straight game, beating Vance and moving two and a half games ahead of the Reds, Brooklyn was in third place, and Doak was on his way to eleven wins. In July, Nap Rucker, now scouting for the Robins, found Rube Ehrhardt in the Florida State League. He reported directly to Ebbets Field, put on a uniform, and won his debut start. A few days later he pitched a shutout. By mid-August he had won five straight. Then, despite a succession of what in today's charitable lexicon are called "quality starts," he collected no more wins while registering three losses. He started nine games, completed six, and fashioned a 2.26 ERA to Vance's league-leading 2.16.

Wheat forecast a great future for the 6-foot-2, 190-pound righthander. "He's a real pitcher," said Zack. "In another season or two he'll be one of the greatest in the country." Ehrhardt did not live up to Wheat's expectations. A starter with a losing record the next year, he faded into the bullpen as a mop-up man and was gone by 1928. But in 1924, if Brooklyn had had either Ehrhardt or Doak for a full season, the pennant might have flown over Ebbets Field again.

The pitcher of the year was Vance, Vance, Vance. His strikeouts dominated the national interest and he was on pace to win thirty. On August 1 he stood at 17-4 after he shut out the Cubs, 4-0, and fanned fourteen batters. That tied his own single-game strikeout mark, set the season before. Along the way Dazzy fanned seven in a row, tying a dubious record. (Hod Eller of the Cincinnati Reds had fanned seven of the Chicago White Sox in a row while winning one of the games of the thrown 1919 World Series.) Vance seemed to be shifting into high gear.

August was as sizzling as Dazzy. The Robins' ace gave an interview saying he lost ten pounds in a game. "I stepped on the scales

The Dodgers' Dazzy Vance, left, was constantly compared to Washington's, Walter Johnson. Vance dominated the National League in 1924 and almost led the Dodgers to a pennant. If the Dodgers had hung on, the two flamethrowers would have met in the World Series.

in the clubhouse before I pitched against the Pirates last week. I weighed 190 pounds in full uniform." Dazzy reckoned about three pounds covered what he wore. He said, "After the game I had a shower and stepped on the scales. I weighed 177 pounds stripped."

Vance explained his hot-weather regimen: "I never drink water during a game. I used to drink water, but found I got better results when I didn't. I lose weight when I am pitching, but between games I get back all I lost and sometimes increase my weight. Last fall when I went home I weighed 201 pounds and that was about eighteen pounds more than I weighed when I reported for spring training. When I started to train this year I weighed 182."

Vance reached twenty wins on August 14, shutting out the Reds, 5-0, on three hits. Fanning eight men, his total reached 177. A week later, he broke his own NL record with fifteen strikeouts. Rube Waddell held the AL record of 16, set in 1908. Vance had fallen behind, 5-1, after three innings, but held the Cubs scoreless through the final six innings while the Robins rallied for a 6-5 win. It was his twenty-second victory and tenth in a row.

With Vance at the throttle, Robinson's express rolled on. In early September, Vance nailed his twelfth straight and twenty-fourth of the year. Two days later, in the morning game of a Saturday double-header, Bill Doak shut out Boston, 1-0, to push the Robins into first place with their fifteenth win in a row. They held the lead only through the lunch break, losing the second game, 5-4, and falling back to third place, in a virtual tie with the Giants and Pirates.

Brooklyn fans were in a frenzy of anticipation on Sunday, September 7, when the Giants, now a half-game ahead, came to Ebbets Field. The streets were packed with fans clamoring to get into the sold-out ballpark. The police could not control them. When a group even more determined than the rest used a telephone pole to batter open the center field gates, another 7,000 people poured in. There was no place in the stands for them so they stood along the outfield walls, a crescent of partisan humanity. Eleven ground-rule doubles were hit into the crowd, but the most dramatic involvement of the mob came while the Robins were rallying in the ninth inning, trying to overcome a Giants lead. Eddie Brown lifted a deep fly to center field. The crowd parted like the Red Sea before Moses to let Hack Wilson pursue the ball. Then they closed ranks and Wilson disappeared. First his cap came sailing out, then his glove, and finally he staggered free, his uniform in tatters. He did not have the ball. It was in someone's pocket.

McGraw fumed, claiming the batter was out because of fan interference, but the umpires ruled it a ground-rule double, leaving the tying and winning runners on second and third with two out. There was a chance for more heroics, but Dutch Ruether, hitting for Johnny Mitchell, struck out. In retrospect, this was the decisive game of the season. Although the Robins continued to play at a torrid pace, so did the Giants.

Brooklyn went to the Polo Grounds on Monday. They pulled back to within a half-game of the top as Vance won his twenty-fifth game and thirteenth in a row. He notched his fourteenth consecutive win by shutting out the Reds, 2-0, in his next start. The margin between the Robins and the first-place Giants remained maddeningly narrow.

The Robins suffered a one-man assault by Sunny Jim Bottomley when the Cardinals devastated the Robins, 17-3, at Ebbets Field on September 16. Bottomley had twelve RBI, an all-time record, hitting three singles, a double, and two home runs. To make matters worse for Robinson, it was his own thirty-two-year-old RBI record that Bottomley erased from the books. The clubbing by Bottomley only stopped the Robins for the day. By September 22 they were back on the Giants' heels, a single percentage point behind.

The fans were eager to celebrate the team's showing. These events take time to organize and with the pennant race likely to come down to the final day, the safer date of September 24 was selected. When 30,000 fans jammed the 160th Regiment Armory, the Robins were still potentially a championship team. Maybe they counted their gold watches too early, but the players each received one for a wonderful season. Robinson made a speech conceding nothing to John McGraw. In his forecast, the Robins would edge out the Giants in the final days and go on to win the World Series.

Three days later it was all over. The Giants piddled on Uncle

Robbie's pennant hopes on September 27, clinching the pennant by beating Philadelphia while Brooklyn lost to the last-place Braves in Boston, 3-2. The next day Dazzy Vance ended the season in a blaze of personal glory, pitching a five-hitter and winning his twenty-eighth game, 5-1. Dazzy struck out five in a row at one point and totaled nine to bring his season mark to 262.

With a 2.12 ERA to cap the pitcher's triple crown—wins, strike-outs, and ERA—Dazzy was voted the National League's Most Valuable Player and collected the $1,000 prize. He topped Rogers Hornsby in the balloting by the writers, even though the Rajah had hit .424, which remains the highest batting average of the twentieth century. Jack Fournier won the home run title with 27, to give Vance a win in their bet, too.

In the American League, Walter Johnson, in the twilight of his career, pitched the Washington Senators to their first pennant. He became the nation's most popular man when he won the final championship game. A tense, exciting World Series might have been even better had Dazzy Vance and Walter Johnson matched fastballs.

Robinson signed a new contract with a big raise and, having finally become a millionaire, Ebbets rewarded the players with generous contracts. They had earned the second-place share of the World Series money, too. In partnership with his friend Cap Huston, Robinson bought a tract of land at Dover Hall in Georgia, amply supplied with birds, rabbits, deer, and possum. There was a stream for fishing and marshlands teeming with water fowl. Robbie also enjoyed his grandchildren's visits to Dover Hall, where they rode horseback and had a great time.

Before Robinson could settle down to a rustic winter, there were dinners to attend and honors to bestow and receive. Maybe it was too much celebration. He checked into the Union Memorial Hospital in Baltimore shortly before Christmas for an operation to remove a lesion on one lung, the result of an attack of pleurisy. The hospital stay stretched out for many months. Then, after a short stop at Dover Hall, and accompanied as always when it was time for baseball by Ma, he headed for Clearwater.

19.

THE PASSING OF CHARLIE EBBETS

While his manager recuperated, Ebbets hustled from meeting to meeting, and from one event to the next. Doctors and friends urged him to ease the strain on his weak heart. Finally, after Robinson had left his hospital bed in Baltimore to go to the team's training site, Ebbets boarded a train for his winter home in Clearwater. Both men were anxious for the test of the 1925 season. Were their veterans close to a pennant or closer to wearing out? Urged to rest in Clearwater after spring training, Ebbets traveled to New York for opening day. The night after he checked into his suite at the elegant Waldorf-Astoria—April 18—he died quietly in his sleep at sixty-six.

A weeping Robinson paid his respects to the Ebbets family. It was decided to play the opening game that afternoon. "Charlie wouldn't have wanted the fans to miss the game," was the excuse. No one observed that Charlie would not have wanted to pass up a sold-out season opener with the Giants.

National League president John Heydler closed all ball parks on April 21, the day of the funeral. Ebbets, often ridiculed for his tightfistedness and his self-importance, had been a successful owner and a good baseball man. He was also an innovator. At the last meeting of the major leagues he attended, he had persuaded the others to agree to play future World Series games on a 2-3-2 basis, an arrangement that remains in place to this day.

It was assumed that Ed McKeever, the younger of the brothers who were Ebbets' partners and the one who had been actively interested in the business, would become club president.

Robinson was an honorary pall bearer at the Ebbets funeral in the Episcopal Church of the Holy Trinity in downtown Brooklyn. From there the long cortege traveled past places Ebbets had known. It passed the boarded-up Washington Park where he had sold scorecards and gained a start in office management. It wound through Grand Army Plaza, along Eastern Parkway, down Bedford Avenue to pass the ball park which bore his name, eventually to wind through the gates of Greenwood Cemetery. The mourners shivered under a driving, icy rain and huddled around a grave which had been dug too small for the ornate, oversized coffin. They stood in the rain and watched for over an hour as the grave was enlarged. Ed McKeever, chilled and sniffling with a cold, went home to bed. In the morning the cold had become pneumonia. Within a week, death again struck the leadership of the Brooklyn Baseball Club.

Ebbets' heirs waited until a hospitalized Steve McKeever was too ill to attend, then called a directors meeting at which they voted Wilbert Robinson a new contract as president and manager for three years with a raise in salary. They wanted Robbie to lead the club because he had worked so well with Ebbets for so long. They felt he would continue the tradition of canny management and low-overhead success that would let old Charlie rest in peace in Greenwood. Instead, Ebbets must frequently have spun in his widened grave during the seasons to come. The era of the Daffy Dodgers under the erratic leadership of Uncle Robbie was about to begin. It lasted only from 1925 through 1929, but even now its buffoonery overshadows Robinson's reputation for sound baseball leadership.

President Wilbert Robinson began his term of office watching from a box seat. He took off the XXL Brooklyn uniform and named Zack Wheat assistant manager, apparently to run the club on the field. Jack Fournier was appointed team captain. After several fretful weeks, Robbie moved back to the bench, though he retained the business suit and could not go on the coaching lines or waddle out to explain errors in judgment to umpires. He resumed signaling the players, positioning them and giving signs. The players were confused. So was Wheat. What did an assistant manager do? In time, Robbie put on a uniform again and resumed field leadership.

Given Robinson's history as a tough, canny, successful baseball man, generally liked if not loved by his players, the phenomenon of the indifferent, undisciplined Daffy Dodgers requires an explanation. Only one makes sense. Although baseball people, writers, and the leaders of other teams expected Wilbert Robinson to handle the dual roles he had been handed, he could not. Trying to do both jobs confused him and everyone else. His presidential duties distracted his attention from the field. And hanging over all of this was the wrath of Steve McKeever, who was livid at being euchred out of the presidency. A self-made man, he coveted the approval of the establishment and cringed at the image the Dodgers developed under Robinson's leadership. He vowed to fire the manager as soon as he became club president, which he expected to be soon.

Under this pressure, Robinson's easy self-assurance, resourcefulness, patience, and guile transmogrified into a sort of bizarre inconsistency. Players lost confidence in his judgment and, perhaps most important, the press pursued this angle so unrelentingly that Uncle Robbie and the Daffy Dodgers became one of baseball's enduring legends.

Given the Dodgers' perennial inability to afford a core of great players, the question about the 1925 Robins was familiar: is this a team needing only a player or two to win the pennant, or one of creaking veterans ready to fall apart? The answer hinged on one fact that gradually became apparent. Vance could win and Grimes couldn't. Dazzy again led the league in victories with twenty-two. Burleigh led the league in losses with nineteen. In between, the rest of the staff registered results ranging from mediocre to disastrous. The promise of Rube Ehrhardt went unfulfilled. Bill Doak spat on the ball a final time and faded away. He left behind a legacy, however. He had designed a revolutionary glove with a shaped pocket. His facsimile signature identified the "Bill Doak glove" for coming generations of ballplayers.

Vance narrowly missed being the first ever to pitch successive no-hitters. He pitched a 10-1 no-hit game on September 8, and five days later gave up only a second-inning single. Grimes often blamed teammates for his losses. In September he had only himself to blame when he lost, 3-2, to the Cubs in twelve innings. His good pitching was undone by his batting. He hit into two double plays and one triple play.

After the near miss in 1924, the Robins dropped to sixth place in 1925. For the next four seasons they continued to occupy that low rung as though they owned it or, at least, had a renewable lease on it.. The Brooklyn *Eagle*, however, was not willing to concede them their customary spot. OVERCONFIDENCE MAY COST DODGERS SIXTH PLACE, a headline once cautioned.

Wheat, who had played on more second division Dodger teams than winners, was comfortable enough with the circumstances to hit .369. Fournier finished third in home runs with twenty-two. If he and Vance had made the same bet that they had the year before, they would have tied.

20.

BROOKLYN'S BABE ARRIVES

In 1926 the greatest hitter in Dodger history arrived. He was also the most popular eccentric ever to escape having a baseball bounce off his head. That indignity never happened to Babe Herman, although writers on the Daffy Dodgers bandwagon said it did. "Shoulders don't count," shrugged the angular, 6-foot-4 Herman, dismissing all such charges.

There was no question about Herman's batting. But he was a terrible fielder who had been passed over by other major league teams because of his defensive lapses. He couldn't catch the ball and, although he had a strong arm, he seldom hit the target he was aiming at. Fans behind third base feared any play that called for Herman to try to catch a runner at the hot corner, because they would often have to dodge a bullet fired into the seats.

Fournier was asked to be Herman's mentor at first base. The Babe did not prove to be much of a student. Although he dislodged the aging Fournier as a full-time player, it was agreed Herman would do less defensive harm elsewhere. The Babe gradually developed into a competent outfielder, but the damage to his reputation had been done. Despite his hitting and power, the writers never let the public see Babe Herman as anything but a clown. This was good copy, but unfortunate for Herman. There are worse defensive outfielders in the Baseball Hall of Fame. In another time, with another team—one not covered by a set of writers committed to portraying the team as humorously as they could—Babe Herman's plaque might now be displayed in Cooperstown. In thirteen major league seasons, Herman batted .324.

The well-known story of three Dodgers on third base begins with Babe Herman hitting a deep fly ball that sent confused runners into delayed action. In a game against Boston at Ebbets Field on August 15, 1926, the bases were filled with Robins. Hank DeBerry was on third, Dazzy Vance on second, and Chick Fewster on first, with one out. Herman's drive hit the left field wall and DeBerry trotted home. However, Vance had held up, thinking the ball might be caught. Running after the catch, he rounded third base and headed for the plate. He was half way there when he heard the third base coach yelling, "Back, back." Dazzy jammed on the brakes and dove back to third where Fewster, chased by the hard-charging Babe, had arrived from first. Herman, smelling extra bases and running with his head down, slid in to join them. The coach, seeing the problem developing, had been yelling to Herman when he shouted, "Back, back." Herman was out for passing the preceding runner (Fewster). Vance was tagged, but he was standing on third, the base he was entitled to by being first in line, so he was safe. Fewster, though, thought Vance was out and that the side was retired. He went to retrieve his glove from behind second base. The Braves second baseman, Doc Gautreau, got the ball and chased Fewster, who ran zigzag patterns in the outfield trying to escape. He was finally cornered and tagged, although he had been out since he left the baseline. The pursuit was a needless but bizarrely appropriate way to end the confusion. The scorekeeper consulted the other writers to trace the play. It is often remembered as Herman tripling into a triple play, but in reality he had doubled into a double play, safely touching second before catching up to Fewster and being called out.

When the story is told, Robinson often plays the part of the third base coach. It makes a better story that way, but he had moved his coaching duties to first base. There were two reasons: it was a shorter walk from the Brooklyn dugout at home and he trusted Otto Miller to give signals at third. But Miller wasn't the culprit, either. He had complained he felt useless coaching third base, because he rarely saw base runners. Mickey O'Neil, a scarcely used catcher, wanted to be noticed by Robbie. Miller agreed and O'Neil bolted out to the third base coach's box at the start of the fifth inning. The manager did not seem to notice the switch. His consent was taken for granted among the easygoing Robins. The debacle was O'Neil's only appearance as a third base coach. Miller was back by the next inning.

Robinson preferred having Otto Miller give the signs. As he got older and more distracted by his executive duties, the manager frequently forgot, or never knew, the signs for such tactics as stolen bases and sacrifice bunts. They had been featured in the play of the old Baltimore Orioles, but he rarely employed them in Brooklyn. His teams were always far behind the league in stolen bases. Bases were stolen and bunts laid down usually on a player's own initiative. As veterans of many major league seasons, they knew what strategy was called for under which circumstances.

One story, which was confirmed later by Wheat, has him coming to bat in the ninth inning with the winning run on first and no one out. In those days, the situation called for a sacrifice bunt, even with the team's best hitter at bat. Zack stared at Robbie in the third base coach's box. The manager searched his memory for the bunt sign. Not recalling it, finally he simply pantomimed a bunt. Wheat, angry that the play had been tipped off by his manager, swung hard. The ball cleared the right field wall. As Zack trotted past third base, Uncle Robbie slapped him on the rump and shouted, "Way to hit 'em, Zack!"

The 1926 season was Wheat's last as a Dodger. His final home run came in a late-season game. The veteran's legs gave out as he tried to circle the bases after hitting a ball over the fence. He limped on his charley horse as far as second and then sat down on the bag. Robinson and the umpires couldn't agree that a pinch runner should be allowed. Wheat sat and massaged his legs for five minutes. Then, in considerable pain, but to encouraging cheers from the fans, he limped very slowly the rest of the way home. Zack retired to his farm that winter but was talked into one final

Silver Fox Jesse Petty, fellow pitcher Jesse Barnes, and young hitter Babe Herman keep their enthroned president and manager company in 1926 or '27.

season with the Philadelphia Athletics by Connie Mack. He played part-time, as did Ty Cobb. Both old men hit over .300.

Wilbert Robinson, the president, was offended by a sports-page cartoon that Uncle Robbie, the manager, would have laughed off. It appeared in the June 5, 1926, New York *Sun*. The season had begun with great promise. Jesse Petty, who had reached the Robins the previous year as a thirty-year-old rookie, had been the best pitcher in camp. Dazzy Vance, who would have started the opening day game, was afflicted with a Job-like case of boils that plagued him all season. Petty pitched a one-hitter to beat the Giants at the Polo Grounds, 3-0. He won his next four starts and led the Robins to first place in May.

Although Petty, called the Silver Fox, was a favorite of Robinson's, his salary was that of a second-year pitcher who had been 9-9 as a rookie. When Feg Murray's cartoon saluted Jesse Petty, it compared what he was being paid with his high-salaried teammates. In President Robinson's opinion they were worth their wages, having proven their ability over many seasons. Besides, what anyone was paid was a private matter between him and the club. Unless it was for news value, such as signing Dazzy Vance to a three-year contract for $50,000, the figures were locked in President Robinson's desk.

The New York *Sun* was the city's most distinguished afternoon newspaper. Its influence was impressive, particularly with the conservative business and banking communities. President Robinson phoned the *Sun*'s managing editor, Keats Speed, to angrily insist his payroll was off limits. Did the *Sun* print the salaries of its executives, its writers, and cartoonists? Such information about individual players, he claimed, was bad for morale. A player like Petty was on a hot streak. If it continued and he had several good seasons, he, too, would be rewarded as Vance and Grimes had been. Robinson claimed Feg Murray wanted the team to rebel and overthrow him. He accused Feg of being a tool of Steve McKeever who, it turned out, was especially rankled by this whole situation.

Keats Speed was outraged by the way he was addressed. The managing editor was cursed by Robinson as though he were a myopic umpire. Instead of a retraction and apology, Wilbert Robinson lost his identity in the New York *Sun*. Joe Vila, the sports editor and columnist, told his staff that Wilbert Robinson was never to be mentioned by name in the sacred pages of the *Sun* again. Further, the Brooklyn club would never be called the Robins. They would always be called the Dodgers. The *Sun* sent back its press passes and canceled its box seats. Coverage would be provided by a writer who paid his own expenses and did not travel with the team or stay at the same hotel. He depended on other writers to feed him stories about the club.

Jesse Petty ultimately won seventeen games in 1926, the most on the staff. He also lost seventeen games, the most in the league. He also figures in one of the classic tales told about the Daffy Dodgers. One hot afternoon, Jesse was resting at the far end of the bench. He fell asleep, softly snoring while the game droned on.

Wanting to arouse his mates to a rally, one player began rattling the bats. "Be quiet," hissed Robbie, pointing to the slumbering pitcher, "Ol' Jesse is trying to get some rest."

There weren't many highlights in '26. Jesse Petty's opening day shutout could be regarded as an achievement, but Frank Frisch's lone hit was typical of the way things fell short for the Robins as the season went on. Rookie Babe Herman did sock nine straight hits over one stretch, falling one short of the record held by KiKi Cuyler (who caught the fly-ball bid to tie the record) and former Dodger Ed Konetchy. Max Carey, long-time Pittsburgh star, was the storm center of a player revolt by the Pirates. Claimed on waivers by the Dodgers, he would eventually succeed Robinson as manager.

On another unusual Brooklyn day, five Dodger pinch hitters all hit safely in a nine-run ninth inning. One of them, Dick Cox, got two hits in the rally, scored twice, and batted in two. Cox is remembered as part of another typical Uncle Robbie story from the era that has been repeated by journalists like Arthur Daley of the *New York Times* and and historians like Dr. Harold Seymour. It goes this way: Oscar Roettger, after several strong minor league seasons, was purchased by president Robinson. He reported but sat on the bench, ignored by manager Robinson. Finally, the manager decided to use his new outfielder. Dick Cox would be benched in favor of the newcomer. The trouble was, not only had Uncle Robbie seemed to forget that he had Roettger on the team, he couldn't remember how to spell his name. After crossing out several false starts on the lineup card, he shrugged, "Ah, well. Cox is hitting pretty good after all," and kept him in the lineup. The story is typical not just because it's funny, but also because it never happened. Dick Cox played only two seasons for the Robins: 1925 and 1926. Oscar Roettger didn't join the team until 1927.

Many of the stories about Robinson and the era of the Daffiness Boys are apocryphal, invented to provide the writers a better story than the day's game. How many Yogi Berra and Casey Stengel anecdotes were invented or applied to them for the same reason? Most of the stories about the team that clowned and stumbled through the years of sixth-place finishes involve tolerant, easygoing

Uncle Robbie. Bizarre things happened to his players more often than to him. That he and his wife would mingle with fans after the game to debate strategy was an act of neighborliness, not self-defense. It might have been viewed as unseemly by Steve McKeever and others, but most Brooklynites loved the Robinsons for it.

And one more thing about those Daffy years: the Robins won more games than they lost at home and played the Giants tough. Robinson didn't win a pennant, but neither did McGraw. In Brooklyn, that mattered a lot.

21.

THE UNENDING SEARCH FOR A SHORTSTOP

Rabbit Maranville was, or had been, the best shortstop in base-ball. He was to defensive play in his time what Ozzie Smith has been in recent years. There are those who deride his presence in the Hall of Fame. They are looking only at his typical infielder's batting marks. They should check the number of times he led in fielding and defensive statistics. With a glove small enough to fit into Ozzie's breast pocket, playing on infields far bumpier than the carpets that gave Smith smooth bounces, Rabbit was the paragon of shortstops. He was also one of baseball's epic wild men. His antic trail in baseball took him from Boston to Pittsburgh, then to the Chicago Cubs, who had a few merry-makers of their own, including the left-handed banjo player Charlie Grimm. In 1925, for some unfathomable reason, Rabbit was made Chicago's manager. His pranks continued and he laughed himself out of the job. In November, Robinson signed him for 1926, hoping that he finally had a shortstop who could hold an infield together. He was wrong. Maranville had almost a decade left in a major league career that began in 1912. But in Brooklyn he lived up only to his hell-raising reputation.

The seemingly backward baseball term "four-for-0" describes a futile day at bat. ("0-for-four" would be technically correct, but that's not what some players said.) On the 1926 Dodgers, Dazzy Vance presided over a band of fun seekers called the "four-for-0" club, who did their best work, not on the field during the day, but out and about at night. Their slogan, frequently slurred, was: "All for one and four for 0."

Maranville was a member as soon as he checked in at spring training that year. He had an extensive knowledge of speakeasies in those Prohibition years. Even more noteworthy was Rabbit's ambition to be a human fly. Hotels in the 1920s lacked air conditioning. Windows were left open to catch any breeze. The players' rooms were usually booked side by side along a corridor. It amused Rabbit to climb out his window, sidle along a toe-hold's width of ledge, and pop in on a neighboring teammate. He would also visit when the occupants were out, transferring a player's favorite razor or a picture of a girl friend or wife from one player's room to another, leading to bickering and accusations of petty theft among teammates.

To hedge his bet on Maranville, who had played in fewer than half the Cubs' games in 1925, Robinson gave up six players to get Johnny Butler from Toledo before the 1926 season. He had complicated internal problems and never fully regained his strength, although he played 102 subpar games at shortstop that year. The hedge proved a good bet. Fed up with the Rabbit's drinking and carousing, Robinson handed him his outright release in midseason. (Branch Rickey eventually straightened out the Rabbit long enough for him to play six more full seasons in the National League.)

In 1928, Robinson finally got a Hall of Fame shortstop: Dave Bancroft. "Beauty" had been a key defensive player for the Giants' pennant winners of 1921-1923. He then went to Boston as playing manager. The Braves were too poor to cover his huge $40,000 salary a fourth season. Robinson was happy to assume its payment and finally have the position played the way it should be.

A number of characters passed through Ebbets Field in the late 1920s, leaving more memorable stories than stats in their wake. Moose Clabaugh was a late 1926 hopeful. When Robinson read in *The Sporting News* that John W. Clabaugh had hit more home runs in the West Texas Association than Babe Ruth's record season total—fifty-nine at the time—by slugging sixty-two round-trippers, the Brooklyn manager was hooked. The dismal season was about to hit the post-Labor Day doldrums of a team headed for sixth place. Robinson thought the Moose would excite the fans into coming out to the last month's games.

They were given teasing glimpses of Clabaugh's power potential. In his debut against the Giants, he pinch hit for the Brooklyn pitcher. Veteran Hugh McQuillan studied the tall, powerful young man. He pitched carefully, bringing the count to three and two. So far, Moose had stood motionless. Finally, he swung. The ball was a blur heading for right field. Bill Terry leaped and came down with the sizzling line drive and stepped on first base for an inning-ending double play. Standing stock still, Moose Clabaugh remained in the batter's box, frozen in disbelief. His hands still held about six inches of his shattered bat.

The next day the Moose was cheered by the early arriving fans when he took batting practice. He responded by stopping the clock. His opposite-field line drive struck the ballpark's prominent time piece where it hung above the Brooklyn bullpen down the left field foul line. The hands, registering ten minutes to two, dropped to half past six. Maintenance couldn't get the clock working again that season.

Inept attempts to catch baseballs hit his way in practice revealed that Moose Clabaugh had never learned this vital baseball skill. Despite coaching by Max Carey, he could not figure out how to judge the flight of a ball. In one game in which he was risked as a defensive player, he ran under a towering fly ball, making ever tighter circles as he closed in for the catch. Alas, the ball came down some twenty yards behind him and the batter had an uncontested triple.

Moose had only one hit in his fourteen at-bats, but it was distinctive. Pinch-hitting in Philadelphia's Baker Bowl, his line drive crashed into the fence where numbers designating the players were hung. A half dozen or so disks fell from the wall, including that of the pitcher who gave up the hit. The Moose had only this cup of coffee in the majors, but he eventually learned to catch fly balls and enjoyed a long career in the Pacific Coast League. He had come up too soon, with the wrong team. The Robins already had Babe Herman.

The reverse image of Moose Clabaugh was the classy little outfielder Jigger Statz (5-foot-7 1/2, 150 pounds) who, although a Dodger only for the 1927 and '28 seasons, was for years the standard by which fly chasers were measured in Brooklyn. Statz returned to the minors and played, mostly in the Pacific Coast League, for many years, eventually appearing in more games than anyone in organized baseball.

It would be hard to overlook Norman "Toad" Plitt, who took his nickname from the similarly-shaped nineteenth century pitcher, Toad Ramsey. Squat and rotund, wearing spectacles and a friendly grin, he could also have passed as a Robinson son. Also known as "Duke," Plitt had been a legend in semipro baseball around Philadelphia. He waddled out to the mound and wheeled up an assortment of junk pitches with an occasional fastball mixed in. Someone suggested that a pitcher who looked so much like the Brooklyn manager was worth a try. Although Robinson vehemently denied that in his youth he had looked like either Toad, he added Plitt to the staff. He started some games, relieved in others, and had a mediocre 2-6 season. He was waived to the Giants and finished the 1927 season winning one game for them. The rest of his career was spent in the highly lucrative Philadelphia semipro circuit.

Robinson was snookered in one trade, going to bed after the deal thinking he had swapped a headache for a star catcher. Burleigh Grimes was serious about playing baseball. He did not relish playing with a team of fools. Pinch-hitting one day, Grimes came through with a double and moved to third on an infield out. The Robins trailed by one run. The next batter hit a routine fly ball to the outfield. Grimes did not tag up. The next batter made the final out.

"Why didn't you tag up and score on the fly ball?" Robbie raged. "You know that guy out there has a weak arm."

"Because I am not a fast baserunner," Grimes responded heatedly. "You should have put someone in to run for me. I'm a pitcher. When you asked me to bat, I did and I got a hit. You should have replaced me then."

The dialogue has been edited of its profanity, but both men were proficient in its use. The argument raged on, down the clubhouse steps and into the locker room, each man cursing the other violently.

Robinson decided to get rid of Grimes, but he wanted a good return and, of course, the one team to which he would not trade Burleigh was the Giants. The crafty McGraw waited until the Philadelphia Phillies had traded their outstanding young catcher, Butch Henline, to Brooklyn for Grimes. Then, while Robinson snoozed the night away, dreaming of his new .300-hitting catcher, McGraw dangled an offer too good for the impoverished Phillies to refuse. Grimes became a member of the New York Giants in exchange for infielder Fresco Thompson and pitcher Jack Scott. Robinson was furious. Grimes went 19-8 for the Giants in 1927. But Ol' Stubblebeard rubbed McGraw the wrong way, too. Banished to Pittsburgh, Grimes won a league-leading twenty-five games in 1928. His still-permitted spitter kept him in the majors until 1934 and his 270 career wins put him in the Hall of Fame. Ironically, he became the manager of the Brooklyn Dodgers for 1937-38.

Butch Henline, even at the price of a Burleigh Grimes, seemed what the Robins needed. A smart catcher, he had a lively bat. Unfortunately, his impressive averages had been made in the Baker Bowl band box. He averaged over .300 for five seasons in Philadelphia, but hit only .237 in three years in Brooklyn. He later became a National League umpire.

Harvey Hendrick, who had failed in earlier trials in the American League, returned to major league baseball with Brooklyn in 1927. He could play outfield and first base, and as a righthanded thrower (though a lefthanded batter), he could also be used at third. His hitting was impressive. He racked up averages of .310, .318, and .354 as the '20s came to a close.

Hendrick is in the record books for a base-stealing feat, although he simply went along with one of the master base stealers of all time, Max Carey. The pair made two double steals in one inning. With Carey on second, Hendrick moved to second base as Carey beat the throw to third. Then Carey stole home while Hendrick took third base. For Carey it was his thirty-third steal of home, and his last.

Robinson relished the chance to snatch a college star from John McGraw in 1928. Overton Tremper was a Brooklyn boy who graduated from Erasmus Hall, also the alma mater of Brooklyn-born Waite Hoyt. He enrolled at the University of Pennsylvania and McGraw spotted him as a promising outfielder. Under a covert agreement, $50 or $100 was slipped to Tremper as a weekend ticket seller at the Polo Grounds. In appreciation, he was expected to sign with the Giants when he graduated. McGraw took too much for granted and was slow to make his offer. When Robinson handed over a $6,000 signing bonus, the Robins had the bright prospect. The college boy was well received by Dazzy Vance and the other blue collar Dodgers, but they offered him no tips on how to play major league ball. In 1927 and 1928 he hit for a combined .220 average as a part-time outfielder and ineffective pinch hitter.

Tremper left baseball for a teaching career. In an interview after he had retired, he told of another connection with Brooklyn baseball. While he was a freshman at the University of Pennsylvania, an upper classman caught him without the beanie cap that all freshmen had to wear. The punishment was a hard spanking with a paddle. Swinging the paddle hardest was a big man on the campus named Walter O'Malley.

Elzie Clise Dudley, whose feminine-sounding name puzzled most Brooklynites, made a spectacular debut. As a relief pitcher on April 27, 1929, he came to bat for the first time in the major leagues and hit a home run. Despite his auspicious start, he lost the game in extra innings. Johnny Frederick came up the same year. He was a star-quality center fielder until a crippling leg injury hobbled him, ending a promising career in 1934.

Also in 1929 Louis "Bobo" Newsom began his eventful career. At 6-foot-3 and 200 pounds, he could be overpowering. Eventually he was, winning 211 games, none of them in his rookie year, however, when he went 0-3. He moved on, a gypsy throughout his twenty-year career with ten major league teams. He even came back to Brooklyn. He missed his time, though. He was cast in the mold of the Daffiness Boys , but arrived too late.

Not all who landed in the Robins' nest during those doleful days that closed out the 1920s fell short of stardom. In 1928 three future stars checked in: Del Bissonette, Al Lopez, and Watty Clark. During the winter of 1929 Robinson traded the popular Jesse Petty for Pittsburgh's star shortstop Glenn Wright. Before he could report to Brooklyn in the spring, Wright had torn up his shoulder muscles playing handball. In 1929 he made only a few pinch-hitting appearances. Then his arm came back for one brief season and he captained the 1930 team that Robinson would lead in one last charge for a pennant.

The final years of the Roaring Twenties, from 1925 through 1929, were a time of national prosperity. The collapse of Wall Street and the start of the Great Depression came as the 1929 season ended. Also ended was Wilbert Robinson's reign as Brooklyn's club president and field manager. In a long overdue settlement between the two factions, Steve McKeever's board ally, Frank York, became president. Robinson's managerial contract was extended for two years, and—back where he belonged—he would refocus and provide one more thrill for the borough. The Daffy Dodgers had had their day.

22.

ROBBIE'S LAST HURRAH

The compromise York presidency brought a truce to Brooklyn's rancorous baseball situation. An unassuming lawyer, York publicly acknowledged Uncle Robbie as the baseball mind of the new arrangement. He would not attempt to become an aggressively involved president as Ebbets had been, and as the Ebbets heirs feared Steve McKeever would have been. McKeever was satisfied that Wilbert Robinson would no longer represent the Brooklyn Baseball Club at the higher levels of league management. Robinson's reign as manager would end, McKeever felt, when the genial and tolerant manager failed to control his players.

York publicly endorsed Robinson, and promised to back him by spending competitively for new players. Then he claimed it was an absolute necessity for the Robins to have a park with a capacity of 45,000 in the immediate future.

Robbie was now a manager without other duties, and in 1930 he had the makings of another surprise contender. The press box jokers would still find material for their columns, but the team suddenly took itself seriously. Some important changes and additions were blending with important holdovers like Vance and Herman.

When Max Carey went back to Pittsburgh as a coach, his place for 1930 was taken by the fiery Ivy Olson. Robinson also took his uniform off for the last time and wore a business suit on the bench. When an umpire's decision had to be challenged, or a pitcher talked to, Olson handled it on the field.

Johnny Frederick set a National League record for doubles with fifty-two. Frederick's lasting place in the record books came in 1932 when, hobbled by the leg miseries that ended his career, he pinch-hit six home runs. One came off the Giants' Carl Hubbell, who was a particular patsy of Frederick's, much to the delight of Brooklyn fans.

In the outfield, Frederick was flanked by the veteran Rube Bressler, who had slowed a bit, and Babe Herman, whose uncertainty on fly balls required that Frederick catch everything he could reach. He averaged 400 putouts in the three unhampered seasons he played. Is that good in a small ballpark like Ebbets Field? Duke Snider, the Hall of Fame center fielder of the Boys of Summer, never came close to 400 putouts. In 1930 Frederick would reach his peak; his first leg injury late in the season left the Robins seriously weakened at a key moment.

The most astounding turnaround for 1930 took place when Glenn Wright experienced what seemed a miraculous cure. After a dismal 1929 season, his first in Brooklyn, when he could only pinch-hit, a surgeon removed a piece of bone from Wright's thigh and grafted it into his shoulder—a radical procedure for the time. By spring training Glenn's throws were hard and true. He played an injury-free season, giving Uncle Robbie the stellar shortstop he had sought all his years in Brooklyn. Wright hit .321 with twenty-two home runs and 126 RBI in Brooklyn's pennant drive.

At second base was an expensive purchase from the Pacific Coast League, Neal "Mickey" Finn. The previous year, Mike Gonzalez, scouting for McGraw, had wired his immortal opinion of Finn to New York: "Good field, no hit." The perfect, succinctly ungrammatical phrase entered the baseball lexicon, although it is rarely attributed correctly.

After the 1929 season other teams, lacking the assessment Gonzalez had provided McGraw, pursued Finn and his Oakland keystone mate, Gordon Slade. Brooklyn outbid all others, only to learn for itself what Gonalez had discovered: Mickey Finn had a great glove and an overrated bat. Finn was rotated with two utility infielders, Jake Flowers and Eddie Moore, at second base. Wright's resurgence kept shortstop Slade on the bench. Finn remained a good-fielding, low-average batter until he was traded to Philadelphia in 1932. The next year, suffering from a stomach ailment, he died after undergoing emergency abdominal surgery.

Al Lopez proved to be a fine example of Robinson's judgment and handling. A fiery kid from Tampa, he was a teenaged backstop for the Jacksonville Tars when Brooklyn played a spring training game in Jacksonville in 1928. Dazzy Vance was the Robins pitcher and the young catcher slammed him for a triple and a double. Alfonso Ramon Lopez was a pepperpot behind the plate and threw out base runners with power and accuracy. The Robins bought him for $10,000, a record price for a Class B player. An old catcher himself, with a team stuck in sixth place, Robinson did not rush Lopez to the major leagues. In 1928 Lopez caught for Macon, Brooklyn's only farm club, and in 1929 he was with Atlanta, which had a working agreement with the Robins. By 1930, Brooklyn had a number one catcher who handled pitchers masterfully and batted .309.

The staff had all the characteristics of a Wilbert Robinson assembly. It was deep with starters, most of them seasoned veterans. When the Cincinnati Reds interpreted a record of 5-16 in 1929 as a sign that Dolf Luque had come to the end of the trail, they cut him loose. Robinson snatched him up. Luque knew how to pitch and could be spotted against certain opponents. Paired with Lopez, the Cuban-born Luque would make up major league baseball's first all-Hispanic battery.

Jughandle Johnny Morrison had been a big winner with Pittsburgh, topping twenty wins and twice pitching the most games in a season, before he drank himself back to the minors. Robinson had rescued him in 1929, and Morrison responded with a 13-9 record. But in 1930 Morrison's thirst became unslakeable. On the team's first road trip to Cincinnati, across the Ohio river from Morrison's Old Kentucky Home, he went out carousing with some backwoods buddies and never came back.

Of course the staff was led by the seemingly indestructible Dazzy Vance. In 1930 his effectiveness returned. His total strikeouts were only four fewer than Bill Hallahan's 177, while his ERA (2.61) was the league's best.

Watty Clark won thirteen but lost the same number. Clark stood 5-foot-11, but Robbie thought he looked too small to pitch in the majors. He stood him back to back with catcher Hank DeBerry to find out how tall Clark actually was. They were the same height. It was later pointed out that Clark was bow-legged and this made him appear shorter on the mound than he actually was.

Dolf Luque's 14-8 mark was the best for percentage. Jumbo Jim Elliott went 10-7 and rookie Ray Phelps was a surprising 14-7. Hollis Thurston, an American League discard, who was ironically called "Sloppy" because he was a natty dresser, won a half-dozen critical games.

Fred Heimach, a midseason acquisition on the recommendation of Casey Stengel, his manager at Toledo, contributed nothing, but added to team harmony. He had already won eleven games in the American Association when he came back to the big leagues. That was all he won in 1930, losing twice for the Robins. A good-hitting pitcher, he batted .258 and was one-for-four as a pinch hitter. Clearly, it was not his statistics that kept him with a pennant contender. It was his tenor voice and piano playing in hotel lobby singalongs when the team was on the road that pleased Robinson. Heimach's melodies kept many of the Robins from wandering off to do deeds of mischief in strange cities. Robinson thought it was good for morale to have the musically talented veteran pitcher around.

It was a well-balanced staff. Five principal starters won in double figures, though no one won twenty. Vance pitched well enough to have reached that plateau but was unlucky. He won "only" seventeen, despite leading the league in ERA, a full point ahead of runner-up Carl Hubbell.

At the plate, the Robins' power would largely be furnished by Del Bissonette and Babe Herman. Now a third-year first baseman, Bissonette, another ill-fated player whose career was shortened by serious injury, had his best season in 1930, batting .336 while scoring 102 runs and batting in 113.

Herman had his greatest season in this greatest of all offensive years.—the one in which Bill Terry hit .401. Hack Wilson set NL records with fifty-six home runs and 190 RBI. The National League as a whole batted .303. Even in this tidal wave of stunning production, Herman stood out, finishing second to Terry with a .393 average, the highest in Dodger history. Without leading in any department, he had 241 hits, thirty-five home runs, and forty-eight doubles. He scored 143 runs while batting in 130.

The Babe even played a better-than-average game in the outfield. He made only six errors in 153 games, and had ten assists. Herman also was impressive on the base paths where other 1930 sluggers were slow-footed. The Babe stole eighteen bases, third in the league. No statistics are kept on bonehead plays, although, here too, the Babe had a stellar season, though some of the antics attributed to him were fictitious or another player's fault.

More than 30,000 expectant fans crammed Ebbets Field for the season opener with the Phillies. The Robins' bats were silent and Watty Clark was outpitched, 1-0. Until Robinson sorted out his team, they played with second division uncertainty. They wasted runs and lost well-pitched games. On April 23 they scored six runs in the seventh inning, but lost 17-16 to the Phillies. On the twenty-ninth at the Polo Grounds, they outscored the Giants, 19-15.

Early in May the Robins began to win, and ran off seven in a row before the defending champion Chicago Cubs stopped Vance, 3-1. Jumbo Jim Elliott got the team going again with a two-hit shutout of Pittsburgh. A week later, he beat the Phillies in one game of a doubleheader while Ray Phelps won the other.

On May 29 the two lefties, Clark and Hubbell, worked a fast 4-1 game, with the Robins beating the Giants in one hour and twenty-eight minutes. The next afternoon, Decoration Day, Brooklyn won a doubleheader from Philadelphia and took over first place. But that was not the story the papers featured. They preferred to highlight a bit of the daffiness that had distinguished the Dodgers in recent years. With Herman on first base, Bissonette hit a deep fly ball to right center field. Herman held up halfway to second base to see if it would be caught. With his speed he could score if the ball hit the fence. The ball cleared the wall just as Bissonette raced past Herman. He was out for passing the runner and the home run was reduced to a single. Guess who was portrayed as the dumbbell by the newspapers? Babe had been playing it safe; Bissonette should have been aware of Herman in front of him. But Babe, despite the great year he was having, was routinely cast in the role of clown. It was a characterization the entire team and its manager fought to overcome. In 1930 the Dodgers were no joke.

23.

THE IKE BOONE FIASCO

The teams expected to challenge the defending champion Cubs in 1930 were Pittsburgh, St. Louis, and the Giants. Brooklyn, at the head of the tightly bunched pack, was a surprise. They caught the nation's fancy as they retained their narrow lead for seventy-five games.

Robinson needed another outfielder. With Bressler, Frederick, and Herman he had a strong trio. Behind them he had the defensively-challenged Harvey Hendrick, and Hal Lee, an untested collegian. Larry Sutton, the Robins' lone bird dog, was sent to the West Coast to scout two heavy hitters, Ike Boone and Buzz Arlett. Both were batting over .400 in the PCL. Arlett had begun as a pitcher but was moved to the outfield to take advantage of his hitting. A good athlete, he could throw and run the bases. None of these were Boone's attributes. A lead-footed fly chaser, he had failed in earlier trials in the American League. So why did Larry Sutton sign Boone when both were available?

The day that Sutton sat in the stands to assess Oakland's Arlett, Buzz got into a heated argument with home plate umpire Chet Chadbourne. The umpire silenced him by smashing Buzz in the face with his mask. This ended Arlett as a prospect for immediate delivery. Sutton settled for Ike Boone of the San Francisco Missions. On paper it looked like a good buy. Boone was hitting

.448 in eighty-three games. The year before he had set an all-time total-base record for organized baseball—553. In the extra-long PCL season, he had hit fifty-five home runs and batted .407. It took time for Boone to cross the country by train and report. Put in the lineup to give the veteran Bressler a day off, his debut was spectacular. Not only did he hit a home run, he made a sensational catch of a ball about to disappear over the fence, leaping, grabbing the ball, and disappearing into the crowd. He emerged waving the ball. The press refused to accept Boone as a spectacular outfielder. He was probably out of position, they reasoned. He had most likely been leaning against the fence when the ball was hit. He had inadvertently been standing in the right place and simply reached up and caught the ball. They were right. Subsequent games proved Boone was a stationary outfielder. Balls hit up the alley in left center had to be chased down by Frederick.

During the summer of 1930 a heat wave gripped the country from the Atlantic Coast to the western plains. Walter Johnson's wife, Hazel, died of heat exhaustion after driving her children from Kansas to Washington. People went to ball games in search of a breeze. In Brooklyn, Robinson managed in his shirt sleeves.

The Robins had reached and retained first place, mostly with four starters. With the arrival of the dog days, Robbie expanded his rotation, giving everyone an extra day's rest. He finally noticed Hollis Thurston sitting in the cooler shadows of the dugout. At the time one of the most popular stage magicians was Thurston the Great. Now his baseball namesake "Sloppy" provided a little magic of his own, pulling two critical July shutouts out of his hat.

The pennant race had continued its torrid pace. First the Cardinals closed in on Brooklyn. Then the Cubs caught fire. By mid-August they knocked the Robins off their first-place perch. Although they battled on, the Robins never regained the lead. In fact, a loss to Pittsburgh dropped them out of the bunched first division. Maybe it jinxed his team for Uncle Robbie to appear on the cover of *Time* magazine's August 28 issue. The national news magazine hailed Wilbert Robinson's accomplishment of leading the Brooklyn Robins to a first-place position just as they were in the process of losing it.

When it appeared that the Robins were ready to fold their wings and head for sixth place again, the pitching took hold. The schedule favored Brooklyn and New York, the eastern clubs playing almost the whole month of September at home. The western clubs, including the contending Cardinals, Cubs, and Pirates, were on the road most of the final month of the season.

Baseball historians should note that on September 12, in a game at Cincinnati, Al Lopez recorded baseball's last "bounce home run." The rule, which said any fair ball that bounced into the stands was a home run, was changed after the 1930 season.

By September 15, Brooklyn had won eleven straight and was nearly back on top of the league. However, it was to be a day when the Robins' lack of outfield preparedness undid them. The game was noted for two events. Once again Babe Herman was passed by a runner whose home run was reduced to a single. This time even the wags of the press absolved Herman of blame. Glenn Wright had hit a low line drive into the gap in left center. Herman, leading off first base, saw the ball skip off the sun-baked turf into the stands for a "bounce home run." He could jog home. However, Wright lost sight of the ball and thought it was in play. Running hard, he zoomed past his teammate. Wright was out for passing Herman, and he also lost to Lopez the distinction of being the last major leaguer to hit a bounce home run.

The most devastating misfortune of the day, however, was an outfield collision between Johnny Frederick and Rube Bressler. Both were seriously injured. Bressler's broken finger ended his season and Frederick's leg injury was the first of the problems that shortened his career. He missed a critical series with the onrushing St. Louis Cardinals, and was subpar for the few remaining games on the schedule.

St. Louis came to Brooklyn for a three-day series that would surely settle the pennant race. The rotation was set: Vance for the opener, to be followed by Luque, and then the surprising rookie Phelps.

St. Louis pitcher Flint Rhem was in the news on the eve of the crucial series. Scheduled to pitch the opening game of the series, he disappeared from his hotel. An all-points bulletin failed to locate the errant pitcher. Manager Gabby Street then gave the ball to his ace lefthander, Wild Bill Hallahan, the rising star, the challenger who had edged out Vance as the 1929 strikeout leader.

September 16 saw one of the most critical games ever played at Ebbets Field. Vance had a no-hitter going until the seventh. Hallahan kept his until the eighth, when the Robins had a chance to break the game open. After the first two batters reached base, pinch hitter Eddie Moore was ordered to lay down a sacrifice bunt. He popped to the catcher, and a quick throw to second base caught Lopez scrambling back for a double play. The next batter was out and the duel went on .

In the ninth, the Cards' shortstop, Sparky Adams, reached third and decided to steal home on Vance's windmill windup. Dazzy reared back and Adams sprinted down the line. He slid untouched across home plate, but the run did not count. The wily Vance, realizing that Adams had too big a jump on him, drilled batter Chick Hafey with the pitch. The ball was dead, Hafey was sent to first and Adams had to return to third. Dazzy then pitched out of trouble and the game went into extra innings.

Remember Andy High? Trade winds had taken him to St. Louis. With a runner on base in the tenth, High was inserted as a pinch hitter. He sent a long fly off the right field wall to score the first and only run of the game. The Robins fought back in the bottom of the inning. Helped by Hallahan's wildness, they loaded the bases with one out. Another walk would tie the game. Al Lopez smashed a hard ground ball to Sparky Adams . The ball took a bad hop but hit Adams in the chest and dropped at his feet. He grabbed it and threw to second. Frank Frisch relayed to Jim Bottomley at first and the game was over. The Robins raged at the umpires, claiming that Frisch had never touched second base. But the Cardinals were in the locker room and Gabby Street's team was in first place—to stay.

The next day Flint Rhem returned, the worse for wear. He was badly hung over, bleary, and unshaven. His rumpled suit suggested that he had been sleeping in it. Rhem's explanation of his absence is a classic baseball story. He had been kidnapped, he complained, by gangsters. They might have been Brooklyn fans, he thought, or maybe gamblers who had bet on the Robins. He had been taken to an empty apartment in Brooklyn, tied to a chair, and forced to drink large amounts of whiskey. When he woke up he was alone. He had managed to slip out of the ropes and escape. Rhem's account of his misadventure was scoffed at, and he was told to sleep it off. Robbie's observation was, "They should have left Rhem and grabbed Hallahan."

Sylvester Johnson defeated Dolf Luque in the second game, 5-3. Johnson never won a more important game in his nineteen seasons in the big leagues. The next day the Cardinals sent none other than Burleigh Grimes to finish off the Robins' hopes. Old Stubblebeard had taken his spitball and grouchy temperament from team to team after leaving Brooklyn. The Cardinals had acquired him midway through the 1930 campaign and he had won big games for them. Now he delivered the coup de grâce to the Robins, winning, 4-3, from Ray Phelps.

The Robins spun into four more losses and dropped to fourth place as the season ended. Hollis Thurston won the final game of the season, beating Boston, 6-3. Brooklyn fans spent the winter groaning about the things that had gone wrong. They moaned about Arlett getting hurt just when he was to become a Robin and the poor second choice of Ike Boone. They wondered what would have happened if Jughandle Johnny Morrison had stayed on the wagon for one more season.

Robinson had put together a strong contender. A break here or there and his final pennant would have flown over Ebbets Field in 1930. The season emphasized that the 1925-1929 Daffy Dodger era was over, punctuated with the exclamation point of an exciting, competitive pennant race.

24.

ROBBIE AND McGRAW MAKE UP

The long-standing feud between Wilbert Robinson and John J. McGraw unexpectedly ended at the winter meeting of the National League in New York City in December 1930. Instead of the frosty nod they usually exchanged, they fell into each other's arms and went off to find a quiet table where they could reminisce. It was a spontaneous reconciliation. With miraculous suddenness, the frigid feelings of the past seventeen years melted in the warmth of an embrace between two aging warriors—both, perhaps, feeling a sense of their own mortality and a desire to put behind them the acrimony that had disrupted their friendship for so long.

Westbrook Pegler, a sports columnist and later an acerbic right-wing political writer, wrote about the two elderly foes making up. "It's a fallacy that old people grow mellow and forgiving," Pegler observed. "In fact, they can take more offense for less cause and exploit the smallest provocations into implacable hatreds than anyone."

Pegler also noted other feuds with seniors that continued to beleaguer Robinson. Joe Vila still banned Wilbert Robinson's name from his paper, the New York *Sun*. To make things more uncomfortable for "the manager of the Brooklyn Baseball Club," his paper sniped away at every miscue or blunder committed by Robbie or his players. Vila had the gleeful help of another aged warrior, Steve McKeever, who was always ready with a public criticism of the manager. Other opportunistic writers joined like a pack of jackals. The goal was to make 1931, the final year of Wilbert Robinson's managerial contract, his last in baseball. The critics demanded a more scientific manager. They had the brainy Max Carey in mind.

Not all of the press wanted to see Robinson go, particularly as a victim of a vicious smear campaign. F.C. Lane, editor of *Baseball Magazine*, wrote a scathing rebuttal in his September 1931 issue. "A campaign against Robbie by a certain section of the New York press, has been quite as venomous as it was ridiculous. This spring an absurd report was spread abroad that thousands of Brooklyn rooters were signing a petition to remove Robbie as manager. The petition, of course, was only the figment of a malicious imagination."

Shortly after the 1930 World Series, Frank York ignored his promise to rely on Wilbert Robinson in all baseball matters. York, acting for the board of directors, announced a blockbuster transaction that brought Frank "Lefty" O'Doul and Fresco Thompson from the Phillies to the Dodgers. A large part of the money that was supposed to be spent on renovating Ebbets Field went to the Phillies along with several players York thought had no future without Robinson to coddle them. O'Doul, a former batting champ, had hit .380 in 1930, and Thompson was the Phillies team captain and a slick second baseman.

The idea of having O'Doul and Babe Herman both in the same outfield was hailed by the press and fans. With Johnny Frederick, whose leg miseries were expected to heal, between the two sluggers, Brooklyn had an outfield that averaged well over .300. Add O'Doul's twenty-two homers to Herman's thirty-five and there was devastating power. Publicly, Robinson welcomed the deal. But O'Doul covered scarcely more ground than Boone's shadow. He had a weak arm and was a slow base runner. The worst part of linking O'Doul with Herman and Frederick was that all were left-handed batters. This meant that only Glenn Wright could provide power from the right side. The Dodgers would be susceptible to good lefthanded pitching.

What really showed that Robinson's influence was waning was the inclusion of Jumbo Jim Elliott among the players Brooklyn gave up. At 6-foot-3 and 230 pounds, the big pitcher was about to meet Robinson's expectations. He had been 10-7 in 1930. To confirm Robinson's judgment, Elliott led the league with nineteen wins for a sixth-place team in 1931, his first season in Philadelphia.

O'Doul and Thompson joined new catcher Ernie Lombardi, bought from Oakland of the PCL. President York had agreed to spend part of spring training in Cuba where a Cuban brewery, noting the battery of Luque and Lopez, offered an all-expense-paid trip to Havana for a series of exhibition games. It is said that Luque, who had played both with and against Cuba's best black players, persuaded management to play only intrasquad games and not risk the embarrassment of being beaten by the integrated locals.

The jaunt to Havana, Prohibition's tourist capital, brought back the days of the Daffy Dodgers. Under Robinson's usual relaxed discipline, the players checked in, threw their suitcases into their hotel rooms, and dashed for Sloppy Joe's and other bistros. Every night was party time. The only daylight many of the players saw was when they had to play a ball game.

Among the Lotharios whose nocturnal hours were spent in pursuit of Cuba Libres and permissive senoritas was an ex-collegian whose courses had included enough Spanish for him to make his way around the bar scene. He was soon in the company of a local lady who joined him in a booth in the hotel bar. Many hours and drinks later she winked and said something that the player translated as "Not on a first date." Determined, he persuaded her to share the next evening with him. This time they rode romantically in a horse-drawn carriage along the Havana waterfront. Then, as a tropical moon slowly sank and dawn broke, the senorita slipped away again.

After a third night of futility, the ballplayer was trying to catch a few hours of pre-game sleep when his phone rang. It was his manager.

"You'd better get up here to my room," he growled. "There's a woman here with a lawyer. I don't know what you've done, but it must be bad. The guy keeps yammering at me in Spanish and the lady just sits there crying. Get up here, pronto."

The player dressed in a hurry and rushed to Robbie's room to find a tension-filled tableau awaiting him. His date of recent evenings glared at him from behind a sodden handkerchief. A tall, thin man in a wrinkled Panama suit, with an unkempt grandee's beard, paced the floor. Robinson reclined in an easy chair, puffing a large black cigar.

Looking puzzled and contrite, the player listened to the complaint against him. Then he nodded agreement and asked, "Robbie, can you let me have ten dollars? I'm short of cash." His manager pulled out a worn wallet and dug out a ten-dollar bill. "This'll come out of your pay check and whatever fine you deserve, too. What's this for?"

The bill passed into the hand of the man in the Panama suit. He broke into smiles. The girl stopped sobbing. Suddenly, everyone was happy. Only Uncle Robbie was baffled by the turn of events. The visitors left, bowing their way out.

"What was that all about?" Robinson wanted to know.

"Just a little mix-up in the currency," the ball player improvised.

Robbie's ten spot had settled the complaint. What he didn't know was that the young lady, who worked in the lawyer's office, had been out so late night after night that she couldn't do the clerical work he paid her to do. Her employer wanted to be reimbursed for wages he paid for work not done.

The explanation given to Robinson was different. "Yesterday I stopped in a shop to buy some things to take back home. I got confused about the rate of exchange and I didn't give the girl enough money. The man owns the store and he wanted the full payment."

"Oh, you can't trust these people," man-of-the world Robbie said, "they'll cheat you every time. You've probably been conned. Well, let it be a lesson to you."

There was an interesting newcomer added to the pitching staff. Clyde "Pea Ridge" Day, nicknamed for his Arkansas home town, was a farm boy who'd been with the Cardinals. He had one eccentricity that amused his teammates: he would rear back and emit a piercing hog call whenever asked. He did it once during a game, having just fanned a batter. In legend, he hog-called after every strikeout. No. Just once. In those days, at least, showing up batters that way would have made him a target for retribution.

A pitcher of far more promise showed up at Clearwater along with a handful of prospects. Robinson looked them over from a rocking chair on the porch of the clubhouse. After watching them throw to coach Otto Miller, Robbie ordered, "Keep the big guy and cut the rest of them loose." The big guy was Van Lingle Mungo, up from two seasons in the deep minors. He would need a season at Hartford in the Eastern League before becoming a 1930s star.

Robinson's forecast for 1931, while not absolutely promising a pennant, claimed the team was the strongest he had ever had. It wasn't. On the field, it looked confused. Strange things happened to the Robins right off the bat. On April 15 a rookie outfielder, Alta Cohen from Newark, New Jersey, broke into the big leagues with a debut that has never been equaled. His achievements needed help from Uncle Robbie, who gave it unwittingly.

It began in Boston where the Robins and Braves were engaged in a ragged, high scoring contest. Babe Herman irked Robinson by ignoring signals to move to a different spot in the outfield. When chastised, Herman said huffily, "All right, send somebody else out there."

"I will." Robbie responded. "Boone, you take over for Babe."

The Robins were still batting and before the inning was over, Robinson had used Boone as a pinch hitter for the pitcher. When the inning ended, Boone headed for right field and was announced as Herman's replacement. However, the score had see-sawed and was close again. Robbie didn't like having Ike Boone defending in the vast spaces of Braves Field. He looked down the bench and spotted Cohen. "Take over for Boone," he ordered and the youngster raced to right field.

This made Cohen a replacement for Boone, who had batted for the pitcher, not Herman. When the Robins came to bat, though, the eager rookie stepped to the plate in the cleanup spot, Babe

Herman's place. He singled to right and the Braves failed to appeal the fact that he had batted out of order. Brooklyn's rally kept going and Cohen's correct turn, ninth in the order, came around. Cohen marched to the plate again and lined his second hit in one inning. Among the beat reporters covering the Robins was a journalist who became one of America's favorite feature writers and book authors. After the game, Quentin Reynolds heard Alta Cohen naively wondering whether anything would be in the papers about his feat. "I'd like my mother to know," he told Reynolds, a writer who was always looking for an angle.

The reporter wrote his game account as a letter to Mrs. Cohen at her home in Newark. In the middle of the night, Quentin Reynolds was awakened by an irate editor at the New York *World-Telegram.* "Where's your copy?" he demanded.

Reynolds insisted that he had filed it hours earlier. He dressed and took a cab to the Western Union office, where he learned the news story had been delivered, as an 800-word collect telegram, to Mrs. Cohen. He never asked who paid for the wire. He only hoped that Mrs. Cohen was happy with her son's performance. The next day, Alta Cohen was farmed out. Apart from two games the next season, his debut game in 1931 was his only major league appearance.

Robinson could not get the cogs of his final Dodger team turning together. When the team hit, the pitching soured. On May 21 his veteran ace Dazzy Vance was literally knocked out of the box while winning the game. He led the Phillies, 3-2, when he was hit on the jaw by a line drive. John Quinn came in and got the final batter. Quinn was, by later reckoning, then forty-eight years old. His career wasn't over until 1933, when he was fifty. Born on July 5, 1883, in Janesville, Pennsylvania, he made a game of hiding his true age, much as Satchel Paige would do a few years later. In 1931, as one of the last legal spitballers, he was still going strong.

Robinson again squirmed while one of his own players, Wally Gilbert, threatened his cherished record of seven hits in one game. The third baseman had a hot bat on Memorial Day as the Robins won a pair of games from the Giants. He had six hits in six times at bat, but failed to get to bat a seventh time. That same day the St. Louis Cardinals also took a pair of games and took over first place. They held it for the rest of the 1931 season. Brooklyn never mounted a challenge.

The Robins played well enough for another fourth-place finish, but, aside from Babe Herman twice hitting for the cycle, the season had little excitement for Brooklyn fans. The end came when Brooklyn won what turned out to be its last game as the Robins, giving Robinson a farewell managerial gift with a 12-3 victory over John McGraw's Giants. It had not yet been officially announced that Robbie's day was done, but the sports pages had reported strife and rancor all season.

That last day, Uncle Robbie and his Robins had the pleasure of spoiling the Giants' Bill Terry's bid to repeat as batting king. The Robins held the Giants slugger to one hit in four at-bats. When all the box scores were counted, he lost the batting title to the Cardinals' Chick Hafey, .3488 to .3486. Sunny Jim Bottomley hit .3481. Brooklyn's .300 hitting outfield? O'Doul was fifth in the league at .336. Babe Herman had plummeted farther, from .393 to .313. O'Doul and Herman were the only Brooklyn batters to top .300. Johnny Frederick batted .270.

The season did not end without promise. Van Lingle Mungo was called up for September after a strong performance with Hartford. His debut is memorable. It bears the lingering stamp of the Daffy Dodgers. The South Carolina farm boy forgot to bring his spikes. The team hunted up a pair of Dazzy Vance's extra-large brogans. Wearing the fading star's shoes, Mungo showed he might yet fill them, as he pitched a two-hit shutout against the Braves. For good measure, he hit a home run and had a single. Before the month ended, he had won twice more and lost a single game. He was Robinson's last major league discovery and kept the heritage alive into the World War II era baseball of the 1940s.

25.

THE FINAL YEARS

After the 1931 season, Mr. and Mrs. Wilbert Robinson emptied their apartment at the St. George Hotel, where they had been living since 1929. As soon as Robbie had said good-bye to his players and coaches, the Robinsons headed for Dover Hall, which was to become their year-round home.

Soon after the Robinsons departed, the club announced the hiring of Max Carey as manager for 1932. Robinson learned about it from the newspapermen who came to see him at his retreat in Georgia. They found him fishing. He expressed surprise at the news, admitting that he had not even known the board of directors was meeting. Other than that, his only comment was, "If the directors want Carey as manager it is all right with me."

Wilbert Robinson was sixty-seven years old. He expressed no anger at the termination of his job. He could afford to be philosophical about the end of his major league managerial career. He had grown weary of mostly Manhattan-based sportswriters who pecked away at him or belittled him, although he was loved and defended by most of the writers. He was, in truth, ready for a life outside the spotlight. No one was better prepared for a life of ease in retirement. He and Ma looked forward to many more years of companionship.

"They had a wonderful marriage," recalled granddaughters Kathleen Gunther and Virginia Harkins. "Ma was friendly but a little naive. One day at the race track they were sitting in a box seat.

Robbie left for a few minutes and when he returned Ma was chatting away with a man she later called 'charming.' She did not know who he was until her husband told her. It was Al Capone."

Their children were well provided for. Son Harry had made his own fortune in construction and real estate. Daughter Mary had inherited her husband's brewery wealth when Frank Gunther died. There were no baseball pensions in those days. The Dodgers voted Robinson a $10,000 parting gift. He didn't need it, but he took it anyway. He had, after all, made the McKeevers and the Ebbets heirs comfortably well off.

Robbie's reputation as a developer of pitchers and his genial personality attracted offers from other teams. But he was content to rest on the laurels he had earned in nearly fifty years in baseball. His cronies from the press and sports world came to visit at Dover Hall. In his first two months of retirement he happily gained twenty pounds, despite warnings from Ma and his doctor that he was dangerously overweight.

Til Huston, his dearest friend, had the answer: get Robinson back into harness, and he would get back into shape. Huston, an owner of the Atlanta Crackers of the Southern Association, named Robinson president of the club. The job of field manager was his, too, if he wanted it.

Robbie accepted the desk job but insisted he didn't want to put his old friend, manager Charlie Moore, out of work. Nor did he want a repeat of the Zack Wheat fiasco of 1925. He stayed clear of the bench. Instead, he installed an exercise bike in the office and rode it daily. He found a bright young assistant, Earl Mann, and made him the team's business manager. Robinson's greatest contribution to Atlanta baseball was to promote Mann, who became a legend of southern baseball leadership.

Wilbert Robinson remained in the front office through the 1932 season and into 1933. Then, in August, with the team failing, he found a uniform that he could still get into and returned to the bench. Moore became his coach. The team won often enough to please him, but his greatest pleasure was, as always, discovering another pitching prospect.

Hugh Casey was his last find to become a star major league pitcher. At 6-foot-1 and over 200 pounds, Casey had the requisite size and heft to attract Robbie's eye. A ruddy-faced Georgian, Casey achieved his greatest success as a relief pitcher in the 1940s, and has the highest relief winning percentage in the record books. It was fitting that Casey's top years were with the Brooklyn Dodgers. He won twice in relief in the 1947 Dodgers-Yankees World Series, when Jackie, not Wilbert, was Brooklyn's Robinson

Robinson enjoyed his later years. Running the Atlanta club was enough responsibility to balance the times he chose to go fishing or hunting, often with old friends from baseball and the writers' ranks. Although he had known that John McGraw's health had forced him to retire in 1932, Robbie was shaken by the news of his fellow Oriole's death on February 25, 1934.

"That is the saddest message that ever came to me," he told the Associated Press. "John McGraw was great as a baseball player, great as a baseball manager, and great as a man. He's had a wonderful career. Baseball suffers an irreparable loss with his death. I can't say enough in his praise, and words cannot express how I feel about his death. Baseball has lost a great leader and a fine man." He said nothing about their long feud, preferring to remember happy times.

In August, Robinson met with Col. Huston for lunch. Robbie was in a pensive mood. "Colonel, you and I have got to go some day. But we've had a lot of good friends and rich experiences. And on days like this I like to call up their faces and think about them."

After lunch he attended a meeting of the Southern Association, where he became dizzy. Helped to his room, he fell, striking his head on the bathtub and breaking an arm as he collapsed. An ambulance was called to take him to a hospital. As his arm was wrapped, he joked with the medics, "Don't worry about it, fellows. I'm an old Oriole. I'm too tough to die."

He was wrong. He had suffered a brain hemorrhage. He lapsed into a coma, with Ma at his bedside holding his old catcher's hand, patting and stroking it. On August 8, 1934, Wilbert Robinson, Uncle Robbie, died quietly, a smile on his face.

Wilbert Robinson at ease. He loved hunting at Dover Hall in Georgia, and spent as much time there as possible during most off-seasons.

When a famous man dies it is commonly said that there will never be another like him. Once in a great while this cliché proves true. Baseball has certainly never seen anyone quite like Wilbert Robinson in the more than sixty years since he died.

Of the hundreds of tributes paid to Robbie, two stand out.

Casey Stengel, the 1934 manager of the Brooklyn Dodgers, said, "He was the finest man I ever knew in baseball and I felt his loss almost as much as if he had been a close relative. I served under Uncle Robbie for seven years. He not only taught me how to play the outfield but he taught me how to live. I regard my after-game conversations with Robbie and his evening fanning bees as the most enjoyable moments of my career. Baseball was its pleasantest with Robbie around."

John Kieran, columnist for the *New York Times*, wrote:

"There may have been smarter managers than Uncle Robbie, but his record wasn't at all bad. His teams won two pennants and were boisterous contenders on other occasions. It is doubtful that baseball ever produced a more colorful figure than the esteemed Wilbert Robinson. Like Falstaff, he was not only witty himself but the cause of wit in others. His conversation was a continuous flow of homely philosophy, baseball lore, and good humor. He was not an intellectual. He knew baseball as the spotted setter knows the secrets of quail hunting, by instinct and experience. A jolly old gentleman and as honest as the sunlight."

Wilbert Robinson, a convert to Catholicism, was remembered with a requiem high mass at Atlanta's Sacred Heart Cathedral. Possibly for this reason, none of his Massachusetts family attended the funeral. Baseball magnates, led by Commissioner Landis, arrived in Atlanta for the ceremony. Col. Huston was prominent among Robbie's old pals who were honorary pallbearers. Mary Robinson, supported by her daughter, Mrs. Frank Gunther, and the Robinsons' remaining son, Harry, followed the casket down the cathedral aisle.

Another of those self-perpetuating mistakes in written baseball history has confused the matter of Uncle Robbie's burial place. At least three publications have identified Sea Island, Georgia, as his grave site.

Actually, after the mass in Atlanta, the body was shipped to Baltimore for interment. There more of baseball's leaders, including National League president John A. Heydler, and Steve Brodie and Joe Kelley of the 1890s Orioles, traveled to Bonnie Brae Cemetery (now called New Cathedral Cemetery) in a cortege of sorrowing baseball men and fans. Wilbert Robinson was buried not far from the resting place of John McGraw.

Mary Robinson died at seventy-four on December 4, 1936, while she was visiting her niece, Mary Ann Healy, in Chicago. Ma was remembered as Uncle Robbie's stalwart supporter during the years in Brooklyn when she would stand with him disputing the opinions of fans about how to manage the Robins. She was survived by her daughter, Mary Gunther, and her son Harry.

In 1945, Wilbert Robinson was elected to the National Baseball Hall of Fame, along with his old Orioles teammates Hughie Jennings and Dan Brouthers. Because of wartime travel restrictions, there was no ceremony or exhibition game in Cooperstown.

Robinson was a major baseball figure for forty years. As a key member of the Baltimore Orioles of the 1890s, he was a cheerful but tough-as-nails ballplayer in what was probably the roughest era the game has ever known.

As a coach for John McGraw, he developed the pitchers on the Giants' 1911-13 pennant winners. As the Dodgers' manager for sixteen years, he fashioned two surprising pennant winners and came close to winning two more.

Despite his successes, Robinson continues to be narrowly portrayed as a confused and indulgent fat man unable to cope with the antics of the assorted clowns, eccentrics, and misfits who made up the cast of his 1925-29 Brooklyn clubs. The stories of balls bouncing off outfielders' heads and three runners hugging third simultaneously were chronicled, embellished, and occasionally invented by a highly competitive group of some of the country's best-known and most widely-read sportswriters. Their writings live on in baseball lore, overshadowing the truth of Robinson's career.

Uncle Robbie, rough but sweet-natured, would probably shrug off this fate, and maybe chuckle at some of the tales himself. Baseball is poorer today for the absence of such men. He and his peers knew what he had accomplished. It is the authors' hope that the reader now shares that knowledge.

SOURCES AND ACKNOWLEDGEMENTS

NEWSPAPERS/BOOKS

Baltimore *Sun* Baltimore *News*
Brooklyn *Eagle* *New York Times*
Sporting News *Sporting Life.*

Bready, James H. <u>The Home Team</u>.
Baltimore: Privately published, 1958.

Brooklyn Public Library
Library of Congress
Maryland Room, Enoch Pratt Free Library
National Baseball Library
North Kingston, Rhode Island Public Library
Providence, Rhode Island, Public Library
University of Rhode Island Library

Hudson, Massachusetts, Historical Society
The Society for American Baseball Research

The authors wish to thank the following for their assistance and support: Frank Fortunato, Rev. Gerald Beirne, Jim Smith, Len Levin, Tom Knight, Dave Kelly, Tom Shieber, Pat Kelly, Tim Wiles, Bill Deane, Steve Lawrence, Jim Reisler, Morris Eckhouse, John Zajc, Fred Schuld and Wilbert Robinson's grandchildren Stan Wilson, Virginia Harkins, and Kathleen Hunter.

INDEX